Going Beyond Google

THE INVISIBLE WEB IN LEARNING AND TEACHING

JANE DEVINE AND FRANCINE EGGER-SIDER

Neal-Schuman Publishers, Inc.
New York   London

Published by Neal-Schuman Publishers, Inc.
100 William St., Suite 2004
New York, NY 10038

The paper used in this publication meets the minimum requirements of American National Standard for Information Sciences—Permanence of Paper for Printed Library Materials, ANSI Z39.48-1992.

Library of Congress Cataloging-in-Publication Data

Devine, Jane, 1947-
   Going beyond Google : the Invisible Web in learning and teaching / Jane Devine, Francine Egger-Sider.
      p. cm.
   Includes bibliographical references and index.
   ISBN 978-1-55570-633-3 (alk. paper)
   1. Invisible Web. 2. Invisible Web—Study and teaching. 3. Internet searching. 4. Database searching. I. Egger-Sider, Francine. II. Title.

ZA4237.D4 2009
025.042—dc22
                                                     2008050850

▶ Contents

▶ PART I
UNDERSTANDING THE DIVISION BETWEEN
THE VISIBLE AND INVISIBLE WEB

▶PART II
FINDING AND UTILIZING THE CONTENTS
OF THE INVISIBLE WEB

▶PART III
NARROWING THE GAP BETWEEN THE VISIBLE AND INVISIBLE WEB

▶APPENDICES

▶ List of Figures and Tables

▶ Preface

"The meaning of life??? How the hell should I know?
Try Google."

Is the meaning of life available through Google? So it would seem from the information-seeking behavior of many students, especially at the college level. In a recent cartoon by Chris Wildt, a guru on a mountaintop sends a petitioner to Google to learn the meaning of life. Wildt pokes fun at the underlying assumption that everything is on the Web and that Google can find it all. In fact, researchers who use only one general-purpose search engine, such as Google or Yahoo!, to find information on the Web are like investors who accept a return of $25.00 as full payment on a loan of $100.00. Even the best search engine offers at most only 25 percent of the information available on the Web.

A vast wealth of information that is not accessible via Google and its analogs is indeed available through the Web. Yet, this vast array of knowledge remains a secret to most students and researchers because general-purpose search engines do not index them. Thus, they fall into what we call the "Invisible Web." The authors (and most librarians) advocate teaching students about the limitations of general-purpose search engines and introducing them to the riches available through other interfaces. Students should receive a fuller picture of the information world in which general-purpose search engines inhabit a small part. They can be encouraged to explore further and to understand the many information choices open to them.

Going Beyond Google: The Invisible Web in Learning and Teaching proposes to address the dilemma created by the explosion of online information available at anyone's fingertips. This book argues that it is up to faculty, teachers, and librarians to fundamentally change "the research process" as currently undertaken by students and redirect learners toward information beyond that found through general-purpose search engines.

It is true that students find one-stop shopping for sources through Google, or other general-purpose search engines, much easier than having to learn and navigate the interfaces of several different publishers. At the same time, commercial firms are also making inroads into the Invisible Web by enlarging the pool of resources indexable by general-purpose search engines. The gap between the visible and the Invisible Web is definitely narrowing. Still, relying exclusively on general-purpose search engines gives the student the false impression that he or she has access to whatever is available on the Internet. It is imperative to educate students to the complexities of research.

Anyone interested in the concept of the Invisible Web can profit from this book. However, the book is specifically geared toward the teaching faculty at every level of the educational spectrum, including librarians who can mold a student's research habits. The first step is to have students attain an awareness of the division between the "surface" or "visible" Web and the "deep" or "Invisible" Web. The next step is to help students find and utilize the contents of the Invisible Web. This objective can be accomplished in various ways, either by requiring an analysis of the sources used or by requiring the use of Invisible Web content for a particular research assignment. The authors present a number of activities that can be undertaken with a class, irrespective of the discipline taught.

To set the foundation for the main argument, Chapter 1, "Characteristics of the Invisible Web," examines its relationship to the surface Web, the nature of the material of which it is comprised, and its searchability. The last section addresses the various constituencies that could benefit from mining the Invisible Web.

Because a discussion of the Invisible Web in learning and teaching cannot be undertaken without an understanding of how users, primarily students, use the Web for research and why they overwhelmingly start, and often end, their research on the free Web, Chapter 2, "Use of the Web for Research," reviews the major user behavior studies undertaken in the past ten years. It is important to identify which features of general-purpose search engines are so attractive to all users, and to students in particular, that they use these search engines to the exclusion of many other sources. Such knowledge can empower teachers and librarians to intervene in the research process to redirect the choice of resources to be used.

Chapter 3, "Introducing Students to the Invisible Web," is a staged introduction to concepts about the Invisible Web that readers can adapt and use in the classroom or the library, irrespective of discipline. Each concept is mapped to the information literacy competency standards of the Association of College and Research Libraries and the American Association of School Librarians. The idea of the Invisible Web can be woven into reference work, library instruction, regular class instruction, and course management software, such as Blackboard.

Chapter 4, "Further Exploration of the Invisible Web," offers structured exercises for more in-depth understanding of the Invisible Web. They can be used by anyone or introduced in a classroom setting.

Chapter 5, "Internet Research Strategies," provides a detailed analysis of a research assignment on microfinance given to a hypothetical second-year student in a college international studies class. The search is run through three search tools: Google; EBSCOhost's Academic Search Premier, a subscription database offered in most college libraries; and INFOMINE, an online subject directory. The results of the three searches are analyzed and evaluated. This type of comparison between the results of two or three different sources can be used in any class where research is required. It forces students to look at the results of their searches and evaluate the validity of the sources found and their relevance to the assignment at hand.

Chapter 6, "A Sampler of Tools for Mining the Invisible Web," examines the different tools, such as directories, databases, and search engines, that teachers and their students can use to explore the Invisible Web. A chart recommending when to use these tools is included.

Finally, Chapter 7, " Visible versus Invisible Web," analyzes the shifting boundaries between the "visible" or "surface" Web and the "deep" or "Invisible" Web. As general-purpose search engines uncover more and more sources by indexing them through crawlers, the border between the coexisting realms of "visible" and "Invisible" are constantly shifting. In addition, new technological innovations are mushrooming, whether in the commercial sector, with new initiatives such as Google Scholar and Google Book Search, or in the library world, with the advent of new library online catalogs such as the one at North Carolina State University Libraries, running on Endeca software. All of these developments have the beneficial result of bringing more content into the visible Web, allowing researchers easier access to quality sources.

Last, appendices include selected additional readings, teaching tools that can be used to impart the concept of the Invisible Web, including graphics, and the text of the *Information Literacy Competency Standards for Higher Education* of the Association of College and Research Libraries.

The authors hope *Going Beyond Google: The Invisible Web in Learning and Teaching* will expand the borders of information beyond resources identified by Google search results and help open a wider world of primary and secondary sources that can better inform learners and expand the horizons of knowledge.

▶Acknowledgments

This book would not have been possible without the support of several people whom the authors would like to take this opportunity to thank. First, we want to express our gratitude to Professor Louise Fluk who was tireless about reading and rereading our chapters and whose invaluable advice was always sought. Thanks must also go to Professor Steven Ovadia who would always drop everything to help with technical advice and know-how. Thanks also to Nasrin Rahman for her great patience with the authors' preoccupation with "the book." Finally, a loud thank you must go to our respective families who lived this experience with us. We will share every success with them.

►Part I

UNDERSTANDING THE DIVISION BETWEEN THE VISIBLE AND INVISIBLE WEB

1

CHARACTERISTICS OF THE INVISIBLE WEB

INTRODUCTION

The Invisible Web presents many problems for the information world, but the essential one for educators and librarians is how to convey adequately its substance and importance. The Invisible Web represents the largest sector of online information resources on the Internet, and yet the first obstacle in discussing it is one of nomenclature. How substantive, after all, is anything labeled "invisible"? The very name implies obscurity and marginalization, which is why some prefer to use the term "deep Web" or "hidden Web" to refer to these resources. No matter how one refers to it, however, the Invisible Web is a phenomenon to be reckoned with.

Simply put, the Invisible Web is the term used to describe all of the information available on the World Wide Web that cannot be found by using general-purpose search engines (Devine and Egger-Sider, 2001). The Invisible Web has various characteristics that can help people understand it. This chapter demonstrates the importance of the Invisible Web by analyzing these characteristics.

Discussion of the Invisible Web should be part of any information literacy program. Knowledge about the Invisible Web should be part of everyone's information and research skills education. Study of the Invisible Web promotes discussions about resource evaluation and how to apply critical thinking to research. It is possible that, if educators present the Invisible Web with the right approach and a clear definition, the very mystique that the name implies will interest and intrigue students. Perhaps educators can even involve young minds in solving some of the technical problems that create the Invisible Web.

Prevailing notions about Web searching, known as Web myths, are worth exploring toward opening a discussion on how to maximize Web research by incorporating Invisible Web resources into the search process. The following are false impressions about the Web and the more complex realities that exist:

▶ *Everything worth finding is already on the Web, or if it can't be found on the Web, it is not worth finding.* Who says so? Why does Web information seem better than information from other resources? The only certainty is that the former can be easier to access. However, the world of information still includes print sources, many other formats, (AV, CDs), etc., and people with expertise.

▶ *Google searches the whole Web.* The overwhelming number of results that users call up with their queries probably creates this mistaken impression. Studies have shown the Invisible Web to be about 500 times the size of the visible Web accessed by general-purpose search engines such as Google (Bergman, 2001).

▶ *The best information is found in the first ten results.* Search engines use formulas or algorithms to rank search results and present them in the order that the user sees them, a process known as relevancy ranking. This ranking may be based on how often a keyword or phrase appears on a Web page or on more sophisticated methods of evaluating linking, as is the case for Google. However the ranking is done, there is no guarantee that the first ten results are the best for the researcher's purpose; only the user can judge. To further complicate the issue, Web designers can create Web sites that will ensure placement in the first ten results. Companies known as search engine optimizers offer this service to businesses seeking good placement.

▶ *Searching is easy.* A saying in the library world acknowledges that "searching is easy; finding is more difficult." The Web has certainly made searching for information more accessible, but "easy" may depend on the expertise of the researcher and how far he or she is willing to take a search. Many use "easy" to imply speed as well, but successful research does require time for evaluation and reflection.

▶ *Everything important is free.* Only in a noncommercial world could one hope that everything important might be free. Information is a commodity and, as such, is expected to generate some profit. People are best served by being good information consumers, and when it is necessary to pay for the information, they should know what they are paying for.

▶ *Everything is truthful, authoritative, and accurate.* Expecting everything on the Web to be authoritative, accurate, and truthful is another ideal scenario that does not exist in the real world. Even with the best intentions of the providers, some information may be tainted with bias, opinions, and inaccuracies. Students and other researchers need to develop evaluation skills to cope with the Web environment.

Similar lists of Web myths have been compiled by Mark Jordan, "Ten Myths of the Internet" (Jordan, 1997), and Mona Kratzert and Debora Richey (1997), "Ten Internet Myths."

RELATIONSHIP BETWEEN SEARCH ENGINES AND THE INVISIBLE WEB

If the Invisible Web comprises all information available on the World
that cannot be found by using general-purpose search engines, then clearly u.
existence of the Invisible Web bears a direct relationship to general-purpose
search engines. We can even postulate that every search engine creates its own
Invisible Web, composed of all the resources that it fails to find or "decides" that it
will exclude from its indexing. Understanding the Invisible Web therefore begins
with a better understanding of how general-purpose search engines work.

In truth, people do not really need to understand the technical aspects of
how search engines work to find them useful; most of us are just looking for
a friendly interface and a few appropriate results. However, a closer look at
how search engines approach the Internet may help broaden one's information
horizons.

Nature of the Relationship

General-purpose search engine developers begin their work by making decisions
about what kinds of information resources and Web sites they will include in their
product. None of the search engines currently in existence are able to encompass
the whole world of Web information. The reasons are many: To begin with, the resources needed to cover the entire Web are massive and prohibitively expensive.
Searching so many resources may also be an unrealistic goal because it would require more time than most users would find acceptable. Search engine creators
make decisions about what content will serve most of their users most of the time.
To achieve their ends, they create computer programs that "travel" around the
Web and index sites according to preset guidelines. These Web-searching programs are called Web spiders or Web crawlers or robots.

In the simplest nontechnical terms, a Web spider starts with a Web site to index
and then searches that Web site for links to other sites. It follows those links and
indexes the sites they lead to and then begins again by looking for more links to
follow. The act of indexing makes those Web sites retrievable as search results. The
spider program follows the parameters that have been set for it. These limits may
involve decisions about what formats to include, how deeply a Web site is searched,
and how often it is revisited. Any limitation means that some information sources
will be excluded. These exclusions form the Invisible Web.

Search engines are created by three essential programs. The spider locates
material to be "indexed." An indexing program captures and stores the material
in a way that makes possible fast and easy retrieval. The final program facilitates
what we as users see on the search screen. This program allows users to enter

ies into a box and it supplies the search results. In effect, the search engine eates its own abridged version of the World Wide Web, which it then offers to its users.

More Information on Web Spiders, Crawlers, Robots

Here are some basic facts:

- ▶ Unless a Web site is linked to from another site, Web spiders may not find it. Web site developers can submit such sites to search engines directly for inclusion.
- ▶ A Web site can establish a nonindexing protocol to ensure that the site is not crawled. Existence of such a protocol means that a general-purpose search engine will not index this Web site. Some of the World Wide Web is composed of private sites.
- ▶ As Web crawlers are designed to follow links from one site to another, they cannot retrieve information from databases, whose dynamic content does not have permanent URLs that can be linked.
- ▶ Each search engine has its own crawler, and many crawlers operate at all times.

For more information about Web crawlers in general see the following:

"All About Search Indexing Robots and Spiders," SearchTools.com, at www.searchtools.com/robots
Web Robot Pages at www.robotstxt.org
Web Crawler, Wikipedia at http://en.wikipedia.org/wiki/Web_crawler

For examples of specific crawlers, see the following:

Google 101: How Google Crawls, Indexes, and Serves the Web at www.google.com/support/webmasters/bin/answer.py?answer=70897&topic=8843
Yahoo's Web Crawler at http://help.yahoo.com/l/us/yahoo/search/webcrawler/

The information resources found by general-purpose search engines are referred to as the "visible" Web or "surface" Web. The term "invisible" represents those resources that, because of their exclusion by general-purpose search engines, are not so easily found. A popular image that shows the relationship between the visible and Invisible Web is one of a fishing trawler with its nets out in the middle of the ocean (Bergman, 2001). The ocean stands for the world of information available on the World Wide Web. The depth of the ocean reached by the nets and the content that they can capture represent the realm of the general-purpose search engine and the "surface" Web (see Figures 1-1 and 1-2). The ocean beyond the nets represents the Invisible Web and all of its possibilities. Of course, the fishing boat can go home with its catch and have fulfilled all it hoped to accomplish without even needing the rest of the ocean. Likewise, the information world as captured by general-purpose search engines is often functional enough for many researchers and their needs. However, as mentioned earlier, studies of the Invisible Web have calculated that it is more than 500 times larger than the visible Web (Bergman, 2001). Other studies find different numbers, but the results still show a tremendous difference in size. The Invisible Web represents

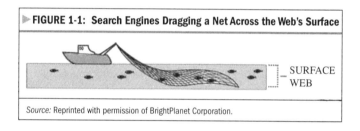

▶ **FIGURE 1-1: Search Engines Dragging a Net Across the Web's Surface**

SURFACE WEB

Source: Reprinted with permission of BrightPlanet Corporation.

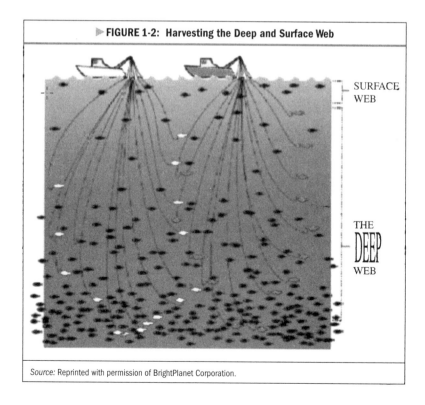

▶ **FIGURE 1-2: Harvesting the Deep and Surface Web**

SURFACE WEB

THE **DEEP** WEB

Source: Reprinted with permission of BrightPlanet Corporation.

enormous information that might be important to the researcher. The researcher needs to know about the existence of this material in order to make informed decisions.

How useful the Invisible Web may be to a researcher will depend on what that researcher hopes to find and how willing he or she may be to continue searching beyond the comfort zone of the general-purpose search engine. What is certain is that when librarians and educators discuss information and research, they need to present the whole picture, not just the surface view.

A Constantly Changing Relationship

As the visible and invisible parts of the Web information world are intrinsically linked, we can deduce more qualities about their relationship. General-purpose search engines vary in which parts of the Web they index and in the proportion of information resources that they offer. Therefore, not only does each search engine create its own Invisible Web of excluded items, but also the size of that content varies from one search engine to another (Sullivan, 2008).

Many search engines, of which Google is a good example, are always adding improvements that enable them to make more inroads into the Invisible Web. At the same time, new information formats that are not necessarily accessible to general-purpose search engines are added to the Web on a regular basis. Such changes add content to the Invisible Web; thus, the nature and size of the Invisible Web are constantly in flux as the Invisible Web adjusts to changes in the search engine world.

Implications of the Relationship

The illustration of the fishing boat on the ocean shows that there is one ocean and that the "visible" and "Invisible" Web are actually parts of the same world of information. As search engines shape the Invisible Web, any discussion of the Invisible Web must be based on knowledge of general-purpose search engines. When librarians and other educators discuss search engines without referencing the Invisible Web, that omission misrepresents the Web information world and may seem to support the Web myth that if a search engine cannot find something, then it is not worth finding. Dissatisfied users of general-purpose search engines may mistakenly conclude that, because they could not find what they needed, it does not exist in the Web information world. The general-purpose search engine is a powerful tool; it does not diminish its importance to present it in the context of the whole information picture.

Characteristics That Make the Invisible Web Important

Size and Quality

The size of the Invisible Web dwarfs the visible Web and that fact alone warrants its consideration; the Invisible Web is simply too large a source of valuable information to ignore. Chapter 7 provides a more detailed discussion of the size of the Invisible Web. The Invisible Web consists of resources not indexed by general-purpose search engines, but that does not mean that it is composed of mere leftovers and unimportant items. Search engines exclude many sources of information because of practical considerations of size, format, and ease of indexing: the limits they set on inclusion are *not* about quality of information. Hence, the information resources located in the Invisible Web have as much claim to quality as anything found by search engines. In fact, estimates show that as much as 95 percent of Invisible Web content is located in publicly accessible Web sites (Bergman, 2001). That means that anyone can use the material if he or she can find it. Databases and Web sites with extensive information contribute the most material to the Invisible Web, and both kinds of resources offer important content.

Fastest Growing Part of the Web

The Invisible Web also grows at a faster rate than the visible Web. The growth rate is easily explained when considering the amount of new material added to the Web every day. Much of that material does not appear as new Web sites but rather appears as content added to existing sites. Databases may appear as only one result for a search engine query but they represent numerous resources and they grow constantly. They also represent quality information. Search engines also shortchange especially rich, deep Web sites, and they also represent large growth areas. Examining the types of materials found in the Invisible Web will help explain its size and growth.

NATURE OF THE MATERIAL INCLUDED

Databases

The claim that a major source of Invisible Web content is databases can be confusing to users of search engines who can affirm that search engines do in fact find databases. However, search engines cannot enter databases or retrieve their content because databases are often dynamically generated. This is a technical point but an important one. When a user enters a search query, the database programming searches and assembles an answer. There is no pre-set answer that can be identified quickly, and the files assembled do not necessarily have fixed URLs. Once the answer results are given and the user no longer needs them, the results are disassembled. They do not remain a fixed entity that can be readily identified or linked to again, as do the results screens of general-purpose search engines. The user will need to reconstruct the search query to get the same results. A search engine spider as a program cannot capture such dynamic information. It functions by looking for fixed answers with URLs. The Invisible Web is created in large measure by technical issues of this kind. Many databases, especially those offered by libraries, are subscription or fee-based. Users must have a subscription or belong to an organization such as a library that sponsors the cost for its members. Most libraries offer a selection of proprietary databases; the databases are accessible with a free library card—one of the best deals in the information world.

Subscription databases are usually designed for target audiences such as students and may be the ideal tool for them to use. They offer authority in their selection of materials, aggregating standard journals and publications for inclusion or utilizing editorial boards of experts to make inclusion decisions. By doing so, databases alleviate some of the user's need to be concerned about the reliability of the information source. By contrast, general-purpose search engines offer no assurance of quality and require that users be concerned with authority, accuracy, and source.

The need for specialization leads to the creation of databases, which enable researchers to tap products specially designed for their area of expertise and need. Databases rely on their own search functions to query content, and these search procedures can be very individual. They pose a problem for the search engine spider that can identify the database homepage but cannot, as yet, fill out search forms and retrieve focused answers. They also pose a problem for the researcher who must "learn" to use the query function. In fact, the researcher may have to keep learning, as he or she moves from one database to another and uses each individualized search form. It is easy to understand the appeal of the simple search box offered by the popular search engines.

Google and other general-purpose search engines are making inroads into this area of proprietary information by establishing agreements with vendors and making listings available through Google Scholar and other such portals. Full-text access to information is still limited, however, to those with subscriptions. In 2008, Google announced that it is experimenting with ways to enable its programming to fill out HTML search forms and thus enable it to capture database content (Sullivan, 2008). If successful, this technology breakthrough will dramatically change Google's relationship to the Invisible Web.

More about Databases versus Search Engines

Databases and search engines have some distinct differences, although they may not be clear to student researchers. In fact, the distinctions may be blurring as the information world keeps changing.

Database	General-Purpose Search Engine
Collects material: Utilizes submission process based on peer review, editorial boards, and other review processes.	**Collects material:** Uses a Web crawler or by submission.
Indexing: Information and data are stored in a uniform way utilizing "fields." Fields allow for the retrieval of specific pieces of information.	**Indexing:** Retrieval is facilitated across several formats.
Retrieval of information: Finds results by matching information listed in fields. All fields are searchable.	**Retrieval of information:** Finds results by searching for keywords found in text. (Relevancy determined by algorithm or similar such criteria.)
Scope: Databases are organized with a special purpose or subject in mind or are intended for a specific audience or membership. All entries in the database relate to its subject, purpose, or some kind of specialization.	**Scope:** General-purpose search engines provide across-the-board coverage.
Authority: A submission process is in place to ensure authority.	**Authority:** Search engine does not evaluate information or Web sites.
Updating: Every day new information can be added to a database easily.	**Updating:** New Web sites and Web content created every day. Search engines are always crawling for new content and revisit Web sites on a regular basis, although frequency varies from one search engine to another.
Cost: Free or fee-based access may depend on membership in a professional association.	**Cost:** Free access.
Examples: ERIC (free); PubMed (free); EBSCOhost (fee-based)	**Examples:** Google; Yahoo!, Live Search, Ask

Deep Web Sites

Similar to databases, Web sites that are very deep and rich in content form a substantial part of the Invisible Web. Search engines set a limit on how much material they index from a site. The "depth of crawl" limitation means that not every page of a Web site will be indexed (Sherman and Price, 2001: 70–71). Information about the exact "depth of crawl" is hard to find, as search engines do not advertise their limitations. At one time, it was possible to find on the Google site the fact that they limited their crawl to 110 K per site, but that information is no longer available. Although Google may have increased its crawl depth, it does not post the information, and it is unlikely that the increase is without limits (Calishain, 2005). This limit means that very rich, extensive, deep Web sites contain regularly overlooked material, and as the site grows, the proportion of material excluded also grows. Examples of rich, complex sites that receive only partial indexing from search engines include government Web sites such as the Library of Congress (www.loc.gov) and the Census Bureau (www.census.gov). BrightPlanet, a company that provides "deep Web" research for the business world, has produced a list of 60 of the "Largest Deep Web Sites" (www.brightplanet.com/infocenter/largest_deepweb_ sites.asp). A review of this list shows open access and fee-based Web sites, the overall preponderance being databases. BrightPlanet reports that the content of these 60 Web sites alone represents 40 times the information found on the surface Web.

Other Invisible Web Resources

Formats

Other varieties of information that form part of the Invisible Web include formats usually untapped by general-purpose search engines. Every format newly available on the Internet requires that search engine producers make decisions to readjust their spider programming to include the new format, develop a special search function for the new format, or simply omit the material. For instance, many search engines offer image searching, but it takes place as a special search option. The basic search may also give results that include images but in a less specific way. The search results will not be images but Web sites to review. These kinds of decisions help create and shape the Invisible Web.

Older formats may also be overlooked, and, again, that material enriches the Invisible Web. A review of several of the search engines can give users a sense of favored formats and excluded formats. Usually, included formats appear on the advanced search page where users may isolate searches according to a particular format. The review should also consider formats that are accessible by special search options, such as images, audio files, and video files.

Forms to Be Completed

Some Web sites, while not presenting themselves as databases, generate dynamic information and present the search engine spider with problems similar to those of databases. For example, sites offering travel directions or job descriptions require information from users. To supply the needed information, they must learn from users where they are and where they need to go or what kind of job they are seeking. Once users supply the information, the site can generate an answer to their query. Again, the answer is created dynamically for the user and disappears when the user is finished with it. The information that these sites create also falls into the "Invisible Web."

Current Material

Very current information and new Web sites represent another elusive area for search engines. Search engine spiders not only look for new content and revisit indexed material to locate changes and revisions but the frequency of crawling and revisiting sites varies from one search engine to another (Notess, 2004). A lapse in time can easily occur during which new sites and new material may go unfound. This type of material may eventually be found and cross over from Invisible Web to surface Web content.

SEARCHABILITY OF THE INVISIBLE WEB

Complexity

A search of the surface Web and the Invisible Web requires searching in two distinct types of environments. The surface Web is created and searched by all-purpose tools, general-purpose search engines such as Google, Yahoo!, and Live Search. No corresponding tool accesses the diverse resources of the Invisible Web. It may be discouraging to the researcher who must learn to utilize many search tools and give more time to Invisible Web searching. Any in-depth research of the Invisible Web will be time-consuming and challenging. Experience can help researchers choose useful tools, but certain elusive items may never be found, even though one suspects they exist. The Invisible Web defies easy solutions, although the initiatives described in Chapter 7 are trying to make it more accessible. Individuals will need their navigation skills in place to mine effectively the Invisible Web's content.

Tools

Chapter 6 covers some of the tools that seem most helpful, but a quick summary of the best resources may be useful here. No one tool dominates but all may be helpful. Some Web tools call themselves search engines for the Invisible Web. CompletePlanet (www.completeplanet.com) and IncyWincy (www.incywincy.com) are examples. Directories such as the Librarian's Internet Index (www.lii.org) can also guide users to Invisible Web content. Most directories are hybrid tools by nature; they list quality information, but they cannot give the quantity expected by search engine users. Guides to Invisible Web content, especially those designed by librarians and appearing on library Web sites, may also be helpful but limited in scope. Using several and a mixture of these types of tools may be the best way to find appropriate Invisible Web content.

Navigation Skills

Finding the right content may also mean digging deeper into likely Web sites. Navigating a Web site requires more than just using its search features. It may require probing the material available and being able to recognize what links can lead to useful information. Also helpful is an understanding of the structure of the Web site. At the very least, users should be prepared to experiment. Site search functions differ. Directories ask the user to browse through successive menus to find material. They usually start with the broadest approach to a subject and then let the user make choices that lead to more specific material. The researcher makes the decisions and does not depend on a computer program algorithm to determine relevancy. Experience usually makes this process easier, but no less time-consuming.

Lack of Stability

Another aspect of the Invisible Web world of information is that it does change all the time and what worked several months ago may not be helpful the next time around. Smart search engine companies are always finding ways to include more "deep Web" content in their own indexes. Invisible Web tools also change and/or disappear. Directories consume many man-hours to develop, yet still can produce only limited access. If budgets decrease or sponsorship fails, they may disappear or become much less effective. All of the problems that affect general-purpose search engine tools also affect Invisible Web searching tools: many kinds of formats and many more materials being added every day.

The Invisible Web is too vast and problematic in nature to be readily accessed. In fact, it inspires a chicken-and-egg analogy: Because it is so vast and diverse, it lacks the desired organization and is difficult to navigate, and because it is difficult to organize and navigate, it remains and continues to grow even vaster and more diverse. Until further technological inroads are made, the Invisible Web will continue to present difficulties for the researcher.

PLACE IN THE RESEARCH WORLD

We can begin with the premise that most people will start any search for Web information by using a general-purpose search engine. Some people, however, may need to take their research further and go beyond those tools to the Invisible Web.

Teachers

These professionals are an important influence on students and the resources they will use for their class assignments and even after they graduate. As discussed in the next chapter, students follow certain patterns in their research and skilled guidance and effective class assignments are required to lead them out of their comfort zones. As is often the case, teachers must stay one step ahead. Educators will also be using the Invisible Web resources for their own research and professional development.

Librarians

Most library users will have already attempted a Web search for themselves before they seek assistance at the reference desk. They will not necessarily feel confident in a reference librarian who appears able to do only the same things that they can do for themselves. Librarians should consider the Invisible Web as the added value that they bring to user requests and be ready to use it effectively—no excuses! Librarians usually have the advantage of subscription databases at their command, selected to meet community needs and often ideally suited to student needs.

Researchers in Any Professional Field

Researchers in any professional field will need to tap Invisible Web content to take their research beyond the level of ordinary expectation. As students progress, their teachers/professors expect higher levels of research skills. That growing level of expertise will include the Invisible Web. Professionals in any field, especially medicine and other sciences, will need to know more than the layperson, and that will require using Invisible Web content.

Dissatisfied Web Searcher

This picture also has a place for the dissatisfied Web searcher. This searcher has tried to use general-purpose search engines to find material that he or she believes should be readily available on the Web but could not locate. Dissatisfaction occurs as a result of frustration and lack of knowledge of alternative ways to search. General-purpose search engines simply cannot always do the job that is needed. Those who have the skills to go beyond search engine resources may find exactly what they want.

Anyone Wanting to Excel

In fact, anyone wanting to excel will want to know about the Invisible Web. People who want to demonstrate that they can produce better and more complete answers to complex questions, who want to be more creative than their peers, will clearly see the advantages of searching the Invisible Web. It becomes a basis for new ideas, thinking outside of the box, and pushing limits.

CONCLUSIONS

The Invisible Web offers a great array of materials that are important for research on many levels. It offers too much valuable content to be left out of the information picture. Only by understanding its potential, publicizing it, and teaching it can informational professionals hope to bring the Invisible Web to the prominence that it should enjoy. Greater demand for Invisible Web resources will hopefully stimulate development of new technology to solve its access issues. To what extent it is part of student and faculty research is examined in the next chapter.

REFERENCES

Bergman, Michael K. 2001. "The deep Web: Surfacing hidden value." White paper. Bright-Planet. Available: www.brightplanet.com/images/stories/pdf/deepwebwhitepaper.pdf (accessed October 3, 2008).

Calishain, Tara. 2005. "Has Google dropped their 101K cache limit?" ResearchBuzz! Available: www.researchbuzz.org/2005/01/has_google_dropped_their_101k.shtml (accessed October 3, 2008).

CompletePlanet. 2004. "Largest deep Web sites." BrightPlanet. Available: http://aip.completeplanet.com/aip-engines/help/largest_engines.jsp (accessed October 3, 2008).

Devine, Jane, and Francine Egger-Sider. 2001. *Beyond Google: The Invisible Web*. Available: www.lagcc.cuny.edu/library/invisibleweb/definition.htm (accessed October 3, 2008).

Jordan, Mark. 1997. "Ten myths of the Internet." *Emergency Librarian* 25, no.2: 66–67.

Kratzert, Mona, and Debora Richey. 1997. "Ten Internet myths." *College and Undergraduate Libraries* 4, no.2: 1–8.

Notess, Greg. 2004. "Search engine statistics: Freshness showdown." Search Engine Showdown. Available: www.searchengineshowdown.com/statistics/freshness.shtml (accessed October 3, 2008).

Sherman, Chris, and Gary Price. 2001. *The Invisible Web: Uncovering Information Sources Search Engines Can't See*. Medford, NJ: CyberAge Books.

Sullivan, Danny. 2008. "Google now fills out forms and crawls results." Search Engine Land. Available: http://searchengineland.com/080411-140000.php (accessed October 3, 2008).

▶2

USE OF THE WEB
FOR RESEARCH

INTRODUCTION

The norm today is for Web users to gravitate toward general-purpose search engines, Google in particular, to initiate their research. Study after study of information users, whether middle school or high school students, undergraduates or graduates, faculty or researchers from various disciplines, shows that a majority of homework assignments, research papers, and other academic informational undertakings start with a Web search engine. Although no one denies the advantages of a tool such as Google, too often the research starts and ends with general-purpose search engines, which are the portals of the visible Web. The Invisible Web, it seems, gets less than its share of attention.

The focus of this chapter is to describe, in greater detail, the Web-searching behaviors of various types of users in educational settings. Before a comprehensive analysis of the importance of the Invisible Web in learning and teaching can be undertaken, it is important to understand how today's user approaches research, specifically which tools are being used and for which purposes.

STATISTICS OF RELIANCE ON THE VISIBLE WEB

Statistics put the picture of Internet usage in perspective. In 2006, 73 percent of Americans had some type of access to the Internet (Horrigan, 2006: 1). In June 2008, according to the Web site Internet World Stats: Usage and Population Statistics, 73.6 percent of the total population in North America used the Internet in some form, and between 2000 and 2008, Internet use in North America increased by 129.6 percent (Miniwatts, 2008).

What do Americans do on the Internet? *Internet Activities* is a compilation of tracking surveys undertaken by the Pew Internet and American Life Project from March 2000 through May 2008. In the May 2008 survey of *Internet Activities*, the first activity listed is "Send or read e-mail," undertaken by 92 percent of the people surveyed in December 2007, whereas the second activity, undertaken by 89 percent in the May 2008 survey, is "Use a search engine to find information" (Pew, 2008). Of those surveyed in January 2005, 57 percent claimed that they used the Internet for "Research for school or training" (Pew, 2008). These Pew statistics do not address the relative use of other resources for research (libraries, databases, print materials).

What tools do people use for Web research, whether for school, for business, or for pleasure? In the most recent report ranking the top five search engines, Google claimed well more than half of all searches in June 2008 (61.5 percent), with Yahoo! garnering a little less than a quarter (20.9 percent), and Microsoft, Ask, and AOL comprising the remaining 17.6 percent (comScore.com, 2008). A 2006 OCLC (Online Computer Library Center) study of college students parallels these numbers: "Sixty-eight percent of college students reported Google was the search engine they used most recently; Yahoo! was used by 15 percent and MSN Search was used by 5 percent" (De Rosa et al., 2006: 1–8). Again, these numbers do not reflect other types of research.

The number of people, including students, who rely heavily on the visible Web for information, with Google as the preferred general-purpose search engine, is enormous. The statistics, however, do not reveal anything about the extent of the use of library databases and other resources, which comprise the greater part of the *Invisible* Web. In addition, to defend the proposition that academic research should not begin and end with visible Web resources, data are needed on the relative value of visible and Invisible Web resources for academic research at various levels. The next section reviews user studies of targeted populations.

USER STUDIES

Over the past ten years, myriad studies have analyzed Web user behavior, each from a slightly different angle. Some studies were conducted at the national level by organizations such as OCLC and the Pew Internet and American Life Project, whereas others are linked to a particular institution. In 2003, Carol Tenopir published a massive report titled *Use and Users of Electronic Library Resources: An Overview and Analysis of Recent Research Studies* that covers the major studies on library user behavior in the electronic age from 1995 to 2002 (Tenopir, 2003). The report analyzes eight major studies consisting of many publications by different authors (Tier 1), and more than 100 smaller studies examined as one unit (Tier 2). Although the thrust of Tenopir's report is research on the use of electronic library resources, quite a number of the studies she reviews touch upon more general user behavior in the electronic age. Because electronic library resources form part of the Invisible

Web, the studies that compare use of electronic resources to use of library collections also touch upon Web use behavior.

The overarching observation that Tenopir makes is that there is no typical user (Tenopir, 2003: 28, 42). Many variations exist among faculty members in different disciplines, among high school, college, and graduate students, gender and age differences, the task, and the type of institution. That said, various generalizations could still be drawn from the various studies regarding the behavior of users in the online environment. The major studies of interest for this chapter are those by OCLC and Pew in which students report that they use the Internet more than the library for research, and that search engines represent their starting point (Tenopir, 2003: 16). Several of the smaller studies in the Tier 2 section point to some general conclusions regarding Web searching habits, namely that students usually choose the first item on a results list, that they enter only one search term in the search box, and that they rarely go beyond the first screen of results (Tenopir, 2003: 34). Carol Tenopir concludes her analysis with the observation that "[c]onvenience remains the single most important factor for information use . . ." (Tenopir, 2003: 45).

Nationwide Studies of College Students and Adults

The 2002 Pew Internet and American Life study *The Internet Goes to College* reports that 73 percent of college students use the Internet more than the library and that their research starts with commercial search engines. "Internet use is a staple of college students' educational experience" (Jones, 2002: 2). The pattern seems to be that the Internet is the starting point, followed by a visit to the library. The study cohort of more than 2,000 college students from 27 academic institutions represents young people who grew up with the Internet and "seem to rely on information seeking habits formed prior to arriving at college" (Jones, 2002: 13).

In the 2002 OCLC study *How Academic Librarians Can Influence Students' Web-Based Information Choices,* 1,050 college students were interviewed and the following results were found: 75 percent of students feel perfectly confident that they can find relevant information for their course assignments; two-thirds feel that they can judge the information culled from the Web in terms of accuracy, cost, currency, and ease of use; 90 percent access the Web remotely. The OCLC study, unlike most recent studies, found that students seem troubled by the inaccuracies of the information retrieved on the Web. These students are also aware that the Web cannot meet all of their information needs (OCLC, 2002: 3–5).

In a 2005 Pew Internet and American Life Project study titled *Search Engine Users: Internet Searchers Are Confident, Satisfied and Trusting—But They Are Also Unaware and Naïve,* Deborah Fallows states that 84 percent of Internet users have used search engines. Most of these users ". . . are very positive about their online search experiences" (Fallows, 2005: [i]). In the 2006 Pew report *The Internet as a Resource for News and Information about Science*, people looking for science news and information use the Internet as their primary source but often verify the reliability of the source either online or offline (Horrigan, 2006: ii, 6).

The 2006 OCLC report *College Students' Perceptions of Libraries and Information Resources* surveyed 396 college students of whom 89 percent initiate their research queries with a search engine compared to 2 percent who begin with a library Web site. However, 61 percent of students have used a library Web site (De Rosa et al., 2006: 1-1), and among students who started with a search engine, 48 percent migrated to a library Web site (De Rosa et al., 2006: 6-3). This study seems to indicate that students' first line of attack in research is the visible Web, but they do not limit themselves to it.

The most recent Pew Report, *Information Searches That Solve Problems: How People Use the Internet, Libraries, and Government Agencies When They Need Help*, published in December 2007, found that "[m]ore people [58 percent] turned to the internet than any other source of information and support, including experts, family members, government agencies, or libraries" to research specific problems such as a serious illness, school decisions, tax matters, changing jobs or starting a business, and finding government programs such as Social Security, Medicare, and Medicaid (Estabrook, Witt, and Rainie, 2007: v). The survey also showed that members of Generation Y, ages 18 to 30, are the biggest users of public libraries when confronted with the problems listed previously (Estabrook, Witt, and Rainie, 2007: vi).

Table 2-1 summarizes the characteristics and results of these Pew and OCLC studies. Although they are not entirely comparable, these studies do show a progression over time in the percentage of students who use general-purpose search engines for research. In 2002, 73 percent of students reported using the Internet more than the library. By 2006, close to 90 percent were reporting that they started most of their research with a search engine. However, signs of thoughtful use of resources also appear in these studies. For example, although 84 percent of people surveyed by Fallows in 2005 used search engines for research (Fallows 2005: [i]), a comparable population faced with specific problems used a variety of resources depending on the nature of the problem (Estabrook, Witt, and Rainie, 2007: 15). Only 58 percent reported using the Internet overall (Estabrook, Witt, and Rainie, 2007: vi).

In a 2006 study commissioned by the Research Information Network (RIN) in the United Kingdom, *Researchers and Discovery Services: Behaviour, Perceptions and Needs*, 395 researchers and 55 librarians were interviewed as to their use of "resource discovery services" (Research Information Network, 2006). The study includes a profusion of charts that analyze the various tools participants use in the course of their research across all disciplines (Google, Google Scholar, colleagues, general Web searches, and various bibliographic databases). Overall results for nine different information tasks appear in Table 2-2 (Research Information Network, 2006: 29–33).

▲ TABLE 2-1: Results of OCLC and Pew Reports User Studies

	Pew 2002	OCLC 2002	Pew 2005	OCLC 2006	Pew 2006	Pew 2007
Author, title of report	Jones, *Internet Goes to College*	OCLC, *How Academic . . .*	Fallows, *Search Engine Users*	De Rosa, *College Students' Perceptions . . .*	Horrigan, *Internet as a Resource for News . . .*	Estabrook, *Information Searches that . . .*
Sample	2,054 college students in 27 institutions	1,050 U.S. college students	2,200 adults 18 and over	396 college students in 6 countries	2,000 adults over 18	2,796 adults
Percentage using search engines for research	73%*	79%	84% (89% of users under 30)	89% (68% use Google)	90%	58%**
Attitude toward evaluation		2/3 feel confident to evaluate info from Web	Only 1 in 6 can distinguish paid from unpaid results; 68% claim search engines are fair and unbiased source of info			
Reliance on other information sources	9% used library more than Internet	61% rely on friends for assistance		67% get links from friends; 61% from electronic sources; 50% from teachers; 33% from librarians		53% rely on professionals; 45% friends; 13% public libraries

* This statistic represents the percentage of students who reported using the Internet more than the library.

** People were asked where they would go to solve a problem dealing with health, school, taxes, or government programs.

▲ **TABLE 2-2: Tools Used for Research Tasks**

Task Tools	Find a Reference	Literature Review	Research New Area	Find Datasets	Find Non-Text Sources	Find Organizations	Find Individuals	Research Funding	Keeping Up to Date
Google	15%	6%	14%	9%	8%	28%	20%		
Google Scholar	78%						22%		
Colleagues			20%	10%	4%	9%	25%	17%	15%
General Web search				11%	17%	37%	22%		13%
Bibliographic databases	35%	34%	31%						
Web of Science and Web of Knowledge*	36%	31%	33%						

* Two of the most used subscription databases.

Source: Resource Information Network, 2006. Reproduced with permission from the Research Information Network.

One of the conclusions of the RIN report is that, although Google is heavily used, it is used in combination with other tools (Research Information Network, 2006: 51). The second most used resources were colleagues and library portals. As in the Pew report on science, discrepancies occur in searching behavior among the researchers of the various disciplines. However, in general, researchers seemed to prefer refining a search from a large set of results rather than looking for precise information, as the possibility of serendipitously uncovering a totally unknown source seemed to weigh heavily with them. As Table 2-2 indicates, roughly one-third of respondents used databases—that is, Invisible Web resources—for the appropriate tasks of finding references, conducting literature reviews, and researching new areas of study. The remaining two-thirds represent a population of researchers who would benefit from greater awareness of Invisible Web resources.

A newer study commissioned by the British Library and the Joint Information Systems Committee (JISC), *Information Behaviour of the Researcher of the Future*, was conducted by the Centre for Information Behaviour and the Evaluation of Research at University College London in 2007. It predicts how the Google generation, those born after 1993, will deal with digital resources in five to ten years. The overarching conclusion is that the future is already here, that "[g]radually, the Internet is sinking into the background as a tool that everyone takes for granted" (University College, London, 2008: 30), that young people, in particular, are lacking in analytical skills, and that "[e]veryone exhibits a bouncing/flicking behaviour, which sees them searching horizontally rather than vertically. Power browsing and viewing is the norm for all" (University College, London, 2007: 21).

Nationwide Studies of Middle School and High School Students

Two studies of younger students by the Pew Internet and American Life Project examine use of the Internet by teenagers as a group and by middle school and high school students in particular. *Teenage Life Online* found that, as early as 2001, 94 percent of teenagers who had access to the Internet used it for school-related tasks (Lenhart, Rainie, and Lewis, 2001: 5). The other report, *The Digital Disconnect: The Widening Gap between Internet-Savvy Students and Their Schools*, depicts how "Internet-savvy students are coming to school with different expectations, different skills, and access to different resources" (Levin and Arafeh, 2002: v). The latter report summarizes how the interviewed public middle school and high school students think of and use the Internet for school. The Internet is considered:

▷ A virtual textbook and reference library
▷ A virtual tutor and study shortcut
▷ A virtual study group
▷ A virtual guidance counselor (Levin and Arafeh, 2002: iii)

These four uses encompass the basic elements of student research: textbooks, libraries, friends, and professionals to offer help in case of need. Indeed, students feel that their teachers are behind in terms of technology, that they hold students back and, most important, that they put roadblocks to their access and use of the Internet during school hours. These Internet-savvy students are completely wired at home and multitasking at all times when online. One student interviewed says: "You can do so many things at once. Like, if I'm on the Internet, I'm researching, doing homework, downloading music, and talking to people, and like, looking at Web sites . . . I do like five things at once on the Internet . . . and that's good" (Levin and Arafeh, 2002: 7). Yet, at school, they can only access certain sites at certain times, provided the school even has computers. To put the importance of the Internet in perspective, when one high school student was asked, "What would you do if you had no access to the Internet?" the student answered, "I get all my information off the Internet. I don't even look at books anymore" (Levin and Arafeh, 2002: 4).

A more detailed analysis of how high school students search the Web was conducted by a social studies teacher, Thomas Scott, and a librarian, Michael K. O'Sullivan, both at Rosemount High School in Rosemount, Minnesota. They found that their students used keywords without understanding what they were searching, with no notion of search strategy or the significance of various keywords. High school students formulate all their searches through a question or a phrase as was once feasible on the search engine Ask Jeeves (Scott and O'Sullivan, 2005).

A paradigm shift has occurred in the way students lead their lives, both academic and personal, and educators, including librarians, do not know how to harness this new access to knowledge that students have and use it in a proactive manner to enrich learning. This is especially true in the realm of research. Students need to be taught how to use Internet sources effectively, not necessarily relying entirely on general-purpose search engines. Teachers, along with librarians, need to re-evaluate their approach to teaching how to do research by taking into consideration the new behavior of today's students. Scott and O'Sullivan stress the need for librarians and teachers to work together to enable students to grasp basic concepts of information literacy before they enter college. The notion of the Invisible Web should be part of that discussion at the middle school and high school level to give students the tools needed to navigate properly the online superhighway. "Unless [both teachers] and librarians educate users about finding information, users will continue to underutilize and misuse information" (Dupuis, 1997).

Studies of Individual Institutions

In "Of Course It's True: I Saw It on the Internet!," Graham and Metaxas write that Wellesley College students trust their favorite search engines even if they do not understand the intricacies of the various search features. Students also seem to place "greater emphasis on the process of finding an answer than on analyzing the actual information" (Graham and Metaxas, 2003: 75). The study consisted of a six-question survey given to 180 students in 2000/2001.

These findings were corroborated by Metzger, Flanagin, and Zwarun in "College Student Web Use, Perceptions of Information Credibility, and Verification Behavior": Students "favor the Internet's capacity to increase quantity, but not necessarily quality" (Metzger, Flanagin, and Zwarun, 2003: 286). The authors studied undergraduates in an introductory communications course at a large public university. Students seemed to be reluctant to verify the online sources they had chosen for their research and they did not seem overly concerned with the credibility of online information. Studied against a nonstudent control group, the college students came across as less concerned about these two issues of online information: credibility and verification.

In "The One-Armed Bandit Syndrome: Overuse of the Internet in Student Research," Richard Barberio (2004) compares the lure of the Internet for college students to the lure of the slot machines for gamblers. Because of the overwhelming information available on the Web, students tune out, get frustrated when they can't find anything, and fail to understand the limitations of commercial search engines. Barberio's study was undertaken in political science classes at SUNY College of Oneonta.

Griffiths and Brophy (2005) report on two studies undertaken at Manchester Metropolitan University in England on search engine use in "Student Searching Behavior and the Web: Use of Academic Resources and Google." The two studies are the Evaluation of Distributed National Electronic Resource (EDNER) Project, concluded in 2003, and its one-year extension in 2004. One of the conclusions of the report is that "[f]orty-five percent of students use Google as their first port of call when locating information, with the university library catalogue used by 10 percent of the sample" (539). The authors make the interesting point that the burden of searching is being passed on by users to the companies that own the search engines (541). Simplicity and ease of use are driving the construction of interfaces. Choosing the path of least resistance, users are giving up their ability to manipulate searches, demanding a simple search box such as Google provides. Griffiths and Brophy talk about the "Googling phenomenon" whereby students expect to search every interface as they search Google (550). They wear only Google lenses and use patterns of library subscription databases compared to search engines provide evidence of this phenomenon.

Not all studies support the finding of overwhelming reliance on visible Web resources. For example, Alison Head reports findings from a small study undertaken in 2007 at Saint Mary's College of California regarding student use of Internet and library resources for research. The small liberal arts college has 2,489 undergraduates and 1,473 graduates, and the student to teacher ratio is 12:1. The sample was extremely small but the conclusions reached run contradictory to most of the research presented in this chapter. The majority of students proceeded with their research using course textbooks or the library's Web site for access to scholarly journals. The third choice was a search engine or an online encyclopedia such as Wikipedia (Head, 2007).

Other Research About Student Information-seeking Behavior

Neil Browne and his co-authors delved into the intersection of critical thinking and use of the Internet in research. In their article "The Importance of Critical Thinking for Student Use of the Internet," they make the argument that students confuse information with knowledge; without evaluation, information cannot be transformed into knowledge. "Thus, the Internet is of value as a research tool only to the extent that the student is willing to practice careful evaluation." They further warn students against confusing ease of access with quality (Browne, Freeman, and Williamson, 2000). Using Invisible Web sources would help students find more reliable information because these sources, found primarily in databases, have for the most part been vetted by scholars and professionals.

Christen Thompson echoes this sentiment in her article, "Information Illiterate or Lazy: How College Students Use the Web for Research," when she says that "The Internet is a pervasive force in today's 'information age,' and while it has many strengths, it lacks an appropriate gatekeeper to filter out the bad information for consumers" (Thompson, 2003: 266–267).

Many studies show the overreliance by students on a single search engine, nowadays mostly Google. In her article "Google as Teacher," Pamela Martin argues that students have come to equate Google with an instructor rather than merely a tool to find resources (Martin, 2006: 100). This same mind-set came through in *The Digital Disconnect*, the Pew study of the high school students who looked upon the Internet as their tutor (Levin and Arafeh, 2002: iii).

In a draft paper titled "How and Why Are Libraries Changing?," Denise A. Troll argues that these are critical times in the need to reach out to students who seem to do most of their research on the Web, do not go beyond the first 10 to 20 items of the results list, do not understand how search engines work or the limits to what search engines can retrieve, and rarely use their advanced features (Troll, 2001). Like Browne and his co-authors (2000), Troll also thinks that students are more interested in access than in quality.

Faculty Research Patterns

A chapter on the information-seeking behavior of students would not be complete without a look at how faculty navigate today's information maze. A direct correlation exists between faculty members' experience with information sources and their expectations of the students in their classes. In 2007, more than 200 librarians surveyed faculty experience with information resources (ebrary, 2007). They found that 89 percent of faculty surveyed used educational, governmental, or professional Web sites for research, class preparation, or instruction; 86 percent preferred e-journals; and 76 percent selected online reference databases (ebrary, 2007: 12, 35). Whereas 53 percent of the faculty surveyed found search engines such as Google a "powerful tool for finding what you need" when doing research or preparing instruction, only 29 percent ranked Google over the print resources of the library (ebrary, 2007: 18, 38). Only half of the faculty assumed that their students would initiate their research in a search engine such as Google, whereas 24 percent assumed that students started research with electronic resources provided by the library (ebrary, 2007: 27, 42).

In a seminal article titled "Using The World Wide Web for Research: Are Faculty Satisfied?," Susan Davis Herring concluded that ". . . although faculty members are generally satisfied with the Web, they question the accuracy and reliability of much Web-based information and the sufficiency of Web resources for research" (Herring, 2001: 213). She noted that faculty in the sciences were most satisfied with the Web, whereas faculty in language and literature were not heavy users of the Web. This survey had 388 respondents in institutions of higher education in Alabama.

In "Business Faculty Research: Satisfaction with the Web versus Library Databases," Nancy H. Dewald and Matthew A. Silvius came to the conclusion that, although business faculty surveyed at several undergraduate Pennsylvania State University campuses reported higher usage of the Web than of library subscription databases for their own research, they were far from satisfied with the results. On the contrary, users of library subscription databases, although fewer in number, were more satisfied (Dewald and Silvius, 2005: 325).

In the CIBER study discussed previously, *Information Behaviour of the Researcher of the Future*, one of the conclusions was that the lack of analytical skills young people exhibit is not limited to them:

> . . . it would be a mistake to believe that it is only students' information seeking that has been fundamentally shaped by massive digital choice, unbelievable (24/7) access to scholarly material, disintermediation, and hugely powerful and influential search engines. The same has happened to professors, lecturers, and practitioners. Everyone exhibits a bouncing/flicking behaviour, which sees them searching horizontally rather than vertically. Power browsing and viewing are the norm for all. (University College, London, 2007: 21)

From these surveys, it seems that, although faculty more and more embrace the use of the Web for their own research, they question the reliability of the information retrieved. There is concurrence that insertion of information literacy instruction into the curriculum is needed, but there is no overall agreement as to how to proceed (ebrary, 2007: 29, 43).

Summary

Joan K. Lippincott sums up the relative importance of visible and Invisible Web resources as follows:

> Students usually prefer the global searching of Google to more sophisticated but more time-consuming searching provided by the library, where students must make separate searches of the online catalog and every database of potential interest, after first identifying which databases might be relevant. In addition, not all searches of library catalogs or databases yield full-text materials, and Net Gen students want not just speedy answers, but full gratification of their information requests on the spot, if possible. (Lippincott, 2005: 13.3; used with permission of Joan K. Lippincott)

Students gravitate toward the visible Web, using general-purpose search engines for various reasons. All of the researchers discussed previously agree on the following factors for the popularity of search engines:

▶ *Ease of use.* Students, as most studies claim, prefer the simple search box of a general-purpose search engine, or, in the coinage of one article, "'the unhindered ease' of a Google search" (Research Information Network, 2006: 59). In their minds, there is no learning curve. Simply type in a search, whether a single term, a phrase, a question, a sentence—whatever syntax the student prefers—and a search engine will always bring up a list of results.

▶ *Convenience.* As long as a student has a computer and access to the Internet, that student can search the Web through a general-purpose search engine. All of the studies examined corroborate the importance of this factor. A student can log on from wherever she or he happens to be, put in a search string, download, print, or e-mail the results.

▶ *Time savings.* Many of the studies report that students place high value on efficiency. If the information cannot be found quickly through a search engine, it is not worth the student's time. Time savings take precedence over reliability of search results.

▶ *Availability of full text.* Search engines offer access to citations, abstracts, and a lot of full-text material. The latter category appeals strongly to all users: the capacity to retrieve a complete article or to access a good Web site from one's desktop makes research simpler, even magical. There is no comparison with having to trudge to a library to get an article or other material.

▶ *Timeliness of resources.* Nowadays, it is not uncommon to access a text online before it appears in print.

PROBLEMS ASSOCIATED WITH USING GENERAL-PURPOSE SEARCH ENGINES EXCLUSIVELY

The five powerful advantages of using general-purpose search engines for research are counterbalanced by the drawbacks of overreliance on tools such as Google, Yahoo! Live or Ask. Most of these pitfalls have been addressed by one or more of the studies discussed previously. The overarching problem with exclusive use of general-purpose search engines is that students are not aware of the limits under which they are working. Research has shown that a general-purpose search engine will retrieve only 16 percent of the resources available on the Web (Bergman, 2001). The rest of the information is hidden or "invisible," 54 percent of it residing in databases that generate results dynamically as a result of a query (Bergman, 2001). Before students launch blindly into a Web search, they should, with the help of their teachers and/or librarians, take a virtual tour of the Web and explore its offerings.

The following sections discuss some of the other pitfalls noted in the various studies of user behavior described in this chapter, classified into three categories: retrieval limits, search strategy limitations, and evaluation issues. Within each of these categories are common issues of time management.

Retrieval Limits

▶ *Retrieving too much information, information overload.* This is a common critique of general-purpose search engines, and even students themselves complain about it (Barberio, 2004; Jones, 2002; Research Information Network, 2006; Tenopir, 2003).

▶ *Retrieving irrelevant information.* Students do not evaluate information retrieved through general-purpose search engines and, as a result, include sources in their research that are not appropriate (Browne, Freeman, and Williamson, 2000; Jones, 2002; Tenopir, 2003; Troll, 2001).

▶ *Not knowing the limitations of a search engine.* Most students have no idea what knowledge base a search engine indexes and, more important, what it excludes (i.e., the Invisible Web) (Barberio, 2004; Graham and Metaxas, 2003; Tenopir, 2003).

▶ *Not realizing that not everything is free on the Web.* Students assume that they will be able to obtain full-text material free, but of course this is not necessarily the case. However, their college or university library will usually provide them with free access to the material through subscription databases. Yet, as research shows, students are reluctant to access materials from anywhere but the general Web (Graham and Metaxas, 2003).

Search Strategy Problems

▶ *Poor searching skills.* A recurring theme in the literature is that students do not take the time to learn about a search engine and how to construct effective searches using that search engine (Graham and Metaxas, 2003; Martin, 2006; Fallows, 2005; Research Information Network, 2006; Scott and O'Sullivan, 2005; Tenopir, 2003; Thompson, 2003; Troll, 2001).

▶ *Rarely using advanced features.* All search engines have a basic search box and an advanced search screen that allows the user to limit searches to a domain, a language, a word, a phrase, etc. Advanced searching is more precise searching and could help students find more relevant material to a given assignment. Still students prefer to work with a single, simple, Google-like search box (Fallows, 2005; Tenopir, 2003).

▶ *Using the same search engine.* Students use repeatedly one familiar search engine. This tendency goes hand in hand with not using advanced features. Students do not realize how search engines work, what the strengths and weaknesses of each particular search engine are, and when one search engine is to be preferred over another. Such knowledge would go a long way toward making students more discriminate searchers (Graham and Metaxas, 2003; Martin, 2006; De Rosa et al., 2006; Fallows, 2005).

▶ *Following the path of least resistance.* This phenomenon has been well documented in several of the studies: students often do only the simplest and easiest search to find sources for their papers (Griffiths and Brophy, 2005).

▶ *Looking only at the first screen.* Web guru Gary Price has taken the concept of the Invisible Web a step further by labeling as "invisible" anything past the first screen of results found through a general-purpose search engine (Notess, 2006: 167). Generally, students do not go beyond the first screen (Graham and Metaxas, 2003; Martin, 2006; Tenopir, 2003; Troll, 2001).

▶ *Getting lost among the links.* Students click rapidly through the various links from a homepage and often do not remember the path they took. The resultant confusion can lead to frustration and the notion that no information is available on a topic.

▶ *Getting frustrated.* To wander around the online world without ever truly finding what one is looking for is extremely frustrating. Rather than look elsewhere, students often quit (Barberio, 2004; Jones, 2002; Scott and O'Sullivan, 2005; Tenopir, 2003).

▶ *Not knowing when to quit.* The reverse of quitting too early is not knowing when to quit. The Web has an alluring, even addictive, pull. Just open a search engine, type in any term, and some results magically appear. Even if the results are not very useful, students do not know when to stop, as it appears to them that they are finding more and more information (Barberio, 2004; Tenopir, 2003).

▷ *Wasting time.* It follows, then, that, although one of the advantages of using a search engine is the speed with which one can access resources, at the same time, it is very easy to get lost in a search and spend an enormous amount of time navigating the Web (Barberio, 2004).

▷ *Overconfidence in research skills.* This phenomenon has been well documented in most of the studies. Students feel that they are skilled researchers and that they do not need any help in obtaining, evaluating, and using online information sources. That a search engine always provides numerous results gives the students the illusion that they know what they are doing (Fallows, 2005; Graham and Metaxas, 2003; Jones, 2002; Martin, 2006; Metzger, Flanagin, and Zwarun, 2003; De Rosa et al., 2006; Tenopir, 2003; Thompson, 2003).

▷ *Seldom asking for help from librarians or teachers.* In one article (Martin, 2006), the author explains how students give Google the role of instructor. This attitude, coupled with the overconfidence mentioned previously, helps to explain why many students do not ask for help with searches from librarians and/or teachers. They count on their friends to recommend Web sites but feel empowered enough to travel alone down the information superhighway (Martin, 2006; Metzger, Flanagin, and Zwarun, 2003; OCLC, 2002; De Rosa et al., 2006; Research Information Network, 2006; Tenopir, 2003; Thompson, 2003; Troll, 2001).

▷ *Preferring access over quality.* Students prefer to use the Internet over other research tools due to ease of access and, in their minds, ease of use, even if other tools provide more appropriate and reliable sources (Browne, Freeman, and Williamson, 2000; Graham and Metaxas, 2003; Metzger, Flanagin, and Zwarun, 2003; De Rosa et al., 2006; Thompson, 2003; Troll, 2001).

Evaluation Issues

▷ *Not evaluating material retrieved.* Evaluation is the hardest task associated with research on the Web. Myriad checklists exist of evaluation criteria such as authority, currency, accuracy, design, bias, etc., but they do not make the task much easier; evaluation of information is, in reality, extremely hard to do (Browne, Freeman, and Williamson, 2000; Graham and Metaxas, 2003; Horrigan, 2006; Metzger, Flanagin, and Zwarun, 2003; Tenopir, 2003; Troll, 2001).

▷ *Not discerning advertisements from real information.* "Sponsored links" and other prominently placed advertising often mislead students, who have a hard time with this aspect of evaluation of information (Browne, Freeman, and Williamson, 2000; Graham and Metaxas, 2003; Metzger, Flanagin, and Zwarun, 2003; Fallows, 2005; Tenopir, 2003).

▷ *Using inappropriate sites.* Even when students make the attempt, they often do not have the requisite evaluative skills to realize that a site might be inappropriate for their particular research, whether the reason is the level of the article chosen or the content of the source.

CONCLUSIONS

The Web has revolutionized the way information is disseminated. It has brought a dimension of connectivity and ease of access that has become the norm in today's society. Still, reliance on the Web should represent one act in the play rather than the entire play. Since "nearly two-thirds of college students say search engines fit perfectly with their lifestyles" (De Rosa et al., 2006: 3–20), it is paramount for educators, whether teachers, professors, or librarians, to insert themselves into students' research process to place the role and use of search engines within a bigger information spectrum. As noted earlier, search engines do not provide access to more than 16 percent of what is available on the Web (Bergman, 2001). Students must become cognizant of this fact and take into account all of the resources available to them rather than simply beginning and ending their research with Google. By introducing the concept of the Invisible Web, educators can acquaint users with new online resources that go beyond the first page of the results of a search engine query.

REFERENCES

Barberio, Richard P. 2004. "The one-armed bandit syndrome: Overuse of the Internet in student research projects." *PS: Political Science & Politics* 37 (April): 307–311.

Bergman, Michael K. 2001. "The deep Web: Surfacing hidden value." White paper. BrightPlanet. Available: www.brightplanet.com/images/stories/pdf/deepwebwhitepaper.pdf (accessed October 9, 2008).

Browne, Neil M., Kari E. Freeman, and Carrie L. Williamson. 2000. "The importance of critical thinking for student use of the Internet." *College Student Journal* 34, no.3: 391–398. Available: http://web.ebscohost.com/ (accessed October 9, 2008).

comScore. 2008. Press release: comScore releases June 2008 U.S. search engine rankings comScore. Available: www.comscore.com/press/release.asp?press=2337 (accessed December 5, 2008).

De Rosa, Cathy, Joanne Cantrell, Janet Hawk, and Alane Wilson. 2006. *College Students' Perceptions of Libraries and Information Resources: A Report to the OCLC Membership.* Dublin, OH: OCLC Online Computer Library Center. Available: www.oclc.org/reports/pdfs/studentperceptions.pdf (accessed October 9, 2008).

Dewald, Nancy H., and Matthew A. Silvius. 2005. "Business faculty research: Satisfaction with the Web versus library databases." *portal: Libraries and the Academy* 5, no.3: 313–328. Available: http://muse.jhu.edu/journals/portal_libraries_and_the_academy/v005/5.3silvius.pdf (accessed October 9, 2008).

Dupuis, Elizabeth A. 1997. "The information literacy challenge: Addressing the changing needs of our students through our programs." In *The Challenge of Internet Literacy: The Instruction-Web Convergence*, edited by Lyn Elizabeth M. Martin, 93–111. Binghamton, NY: The Haworth Press.

ebrary. 2007. 2007 *global faculty e-book survey*. Palo Alto, CA: ebrary. Available: www.ebrary.com/corp/collateral/en/Survey/ebrary_faculty_survey_2007.pdf (accessed October 9, 2008). Data used by permission of Allen McKiel, for ebrary.

Estabrook, Leigh, Evans Witt, and Lee Rainie. 2007. *Information Searches That Solve Problems: How People Use the Internet, Libraries, and Government Agencies When They Need Help*. Washington, DC: Pew Internet and American Life Project; Champaign, IL: Graduate School of Library and Information Science, University of Illinois at Urbana-Champaign. Available: www.pewinternet.org/pdfs/PEW_UI_LibrariesReport.pdf (accessed October 9, 2008).

Fallows, Deborah. 2005. *Search Engine Users: Internet Searchers Are Confident, Satisfied and Trusting— But They Are Also Unaware and Naïve*. Washington, DC: Pew Internet and American Life Project. Available: www.pewinternet.org/pdfs/PIP_Searchengine_users.pdf (accessed October 9, 2008).

Graham, Leah, and Panagiotis Takis Metaxas. 2003. "Of course it's true; I saw it on the Internet! Critical thinking in the Internet era." *Communications of the ACM* 46, no.5: 71–75.

Griffiths, Jillian R., and Peter Brophy. 2005. "Student searching behavior and the Web: Use of academic resources and Google." *Library Trends* 53, no.44: 539–554.

Head, Alison J. 2007. "Beyond Google: How do students conduct academic research?" *First Monday* 12, no.8. Available: http://firstmonday.org/htbin/cgiwrap/bin/ojs/index.php/fm/article/veiwArticle/1998/1873 (accessed December 6, 2008).

Herring, Susan Davis. 2001. "Using the World Wide Web for research: Are faculty satisfied?" *Journal of Academic Librarianship* 27, no.3: 213–219.

Horrigan, John B. 2006. *The Internet as a Resource for News and Information about Science: The Convenience of Getting Scientific Material on the Web Opens Doors to Better Attitudes and Understanding of Science*. Washington, DC: Pew Internet and American Life Project. Available: www.pewinternet.org/pdfs/PIP_Exploratorium_Science.pdf (accessed December 6, 2008).

Jones, Steve. 2002. *The Internet Goes to College: How Students Are Living in the Future with Today's Technology*. Washington, DC: Pew Internet and American Life Project. Available: www.pewinternet.org/pdfs/PIP_College_Report.pdf (accessed October 9, 2008).

Lenhart, Amanda, Lee Rainie, and Oliver Lewis. 2001. *Teenage Life Online: The Rise of the Instant-message Generation and the Internet's Impact on Friendship and Family Relationships*. Washington, DC: Pew Internet and American Life Project. www.pewinternet.org/pdfs/PIP_Teens_Report.pdf (accessed October 9, 2008).

Levin, Douglas, and Sousan Arafeh. 2002. *The Digital Disconnect: The Widening Gap Between Internet-Savvy Students and Their Schools*. Washington, DC: Pew Internet and American Life Project. Available: www.pewinternet.org/pdfs/PIP_Schools_Internet_Report.pdf (accessed October 9, 2008).

Lippincott, Joan K. 2005. "Net generation students and libraries." In *Educating the Net Generation*, edited by Diana G. Oblinger and James L. Oblinger, 13.1–13.15. Boulder, CO: EDUCAUSE. Available: http://net.educause.edu/ir/library/pdf/pub7101m.pdf (accessed October 9, 2008).

Martin, Pamela. 2006. "Google as teacher: Everything your students know they learned from searching Google." *College & Research Libraries News* 67, no.2: 100–101.

Metzger, Miriam J., Andrew J. Flanagin, and Lara Zwarun. 2003. "College student Web use, perceptions of information credibility, and verification behavior." *Computers & Education* 41, no.3: 271–290.

Miniwatts Marketing Group. 2008. "Internet usage statistics: The Internet big picture." Internet World Stats: Usage and Population Statistics. Available: www.internetworldstats. com/stats.htm (accessed December 5, 2008).

Notess, Greg R. 2006. *Teaching Web Search Skills: Techniques and Strategies of Top Trainers.* Medford, NJ: Information Today.

OCLC. 2002. *How Academic Librarians Can Influence Students' Web-based Information Choices.* OCLC White Paper on the Information Habits of College Students. Dublin, OH: OCLC Online Computer Library Center. Available: www5.oclc.org/downloads/community/ informationhabits.pdf (accessed October 6, 2008).

Pew Internet and American Life Project Tracking Surveys. 2008. *Internet Activities.* Washington, DC: Pew Internet and American Life Project. Available: http://pewinternet.org/trends/ Internet_Activities_7.22.08.htm (accessed December 6, 2008).

Research Information Network. 2006. *Researchers and Discovery Services: Behaviour, Perceptions and Needs.* London: Research Information Network. Available: www.rin.ac.uk/files/ Report%20-%20final.pdf (accessed October 9, 2008). Data reproduced with permission from the Research Information Network.

Scott, Thomas J., and Michael K. O'Sullivan. 2005. "Analyzing student search strategies: Making a case for integrating information literacy skills into the curriculum." *Teacher Librarian* 33, no.1: 21–25. Available: http://web.ebscohost.com/ (accessed October 9, 2008).

Tenopir, Carol. 2003. *Use and Users of Electronic Library Resources: An Overview and Analysis of Recent Research Studies.* Publication 120. Washington, DC: Council on Library and Information Resources (CLIR). Available: www.clir.org/pubs/reports/pub120/publ20.pdf (accessed December 6, 2008).

Thompson, Christen. 2003. "Information illiterate or lazy: How college students use the Web for research." *portal: Libraries and the Academy* 3, no.2: 259–268. Available: http://muse. jhu.edu/journals/portal_libraries_and_the_academy/v003/3.2thompson.pdf (accessed October 9, 2008).

Troll, Denise A. 2001. "How and why are libraries changing?" Draft. *Digital Library Federation.* Available: www.diglib.org/use/whitepaper.htm (accessed October 9, 2008).

University College, London. Centre for Information Behaviour and the Evaluation of Research. 2007. *Student Information-seeking Behaviour in Context: Key Findings from CIBER Log Studies.* [Working paper IV]. London: University College London, Centre for Information Behaviour and the Evaluation of Research [CIBER], June 22. Available: www.ucl.ac.uk/slais/ research/ciber/downloads/GG%20Work%20Package%20IV.pdf (accessed October 9, 2008).

University College, London. Centre for Information Behaviour and the Evaluation of Research. 2008. *Information Behaviour of the Researcher of the Future.* [Executive summary]. London: University College London, Centre for Information Behaviour and the Evaluation of Research [CIBER], January 11. Available: www.ucl.ac.uk/slais/research/ciber/ downloads/ggexecutive.pdf (accessed October 9, 2008).

▶Part II

FINDING AND UTILIZING THE CONTENTS OF THE INVISIBLE WEB

▶3

INTRODUCING STUDENTS TO THE INVISIBLE WEB

INTRODUCTION

The Invisible Web is a large and integral part of the Web world of information and should always be presented in discussions of that world. The Invisible Web has its own characteristics, but these make sense only when reference is made to the surface Web. Ideas that can help students understand the surface Web can also help them understand the Invisible Web.

This chapter suggests ways to introduce aspects of the Invisible Web into common teaching and student experiences, both in the classroom and in the library. The ideas and concepts presented here will further understanding of the whole world of Web information and the Invisible Web's part in it.

PREREQUISITES FOR LEARNING ABOUT THE INVISIBLE WEB

Students, educators, and librarians exchange ideas about information and the information world during classroom instruction, through course management software such as Blackboard and in interactions at the library reference desk. All of these interchanges offer opportunities to introduce elements of Invisible Web searching. The nature and extent of those opportunities will depend on (1) what kinds of information are needed; (2) the attitudes, skills, and experience levels of the students; and (3) the time and venues available for imparting lessons about the Invisible Web.

The Information Need

Invisible Web research represents a form of advanced searching. Most searches may still start with general-purpose search engines, and many will be successful without any need to take the search to any extra lengths. The Invisible Web offers rich material that can expand on general search engine findings, but it may not necessarily be the first place to look, nor, perhaps, even the second. Experience will help users decide what kind of information will serve their needs and where they are most likely to find it. The Invisible Web is not in competition with the general-purpose search engines trawling the surface Web, an idea that should be clearly presented in any introduction to the Invisible Web. But given some extra effort by the researcher, the Invisible Web can augment general search engine results and may be the difference between successful research and incomplete results. The information need determines whether the extra effort is warranted. If the need is not there, the instruction about the Invisible Web may fall on deaf ears.

Student Attitudes and Preparedness

As the last chapter revealed, students generally feel positive about using online tools. Their confidence, however, does not always translate into successful search skills, nor does it represent a strong awareness of how the Web information world is constructed. Any use of the Invisible Web needs to be based on an understanding of that world. The Invisible Web represents a complexity of that information world. It exists as a consequence of general-purpose search engines; therefore, knowing how search engines work should be a prerequisite to Invisible Web searching. Students who have very little experience with any kind of research may not yet be ready for Invisible Web research.

Many students have of course used general-purpose search engines and have already learned something from the experience. What they have learned is a factor to consider in teaching about the Invisible Web. In her article "Google as Teacher," Pamela Martin suggests that Google's message makes a strong impression: "Google teaches students what to expect from online searching. It has totally dominated many students' online searching experience, and it forms their online mindset" (Martin, 2006: 100).

Google's most pervasive message is that searching is always easy. The same can be said for other general-purpose search engines such as Yahoo! and Live Search. The message of the Invisible Web is the exact opposite, namely, that searching is complicated at times and may require the use of several search tools, a range of navigation skills, and experience. The easy search may be successful in certain circumstances, depending on the nature of the research, and may seem to validate the impression that it must always be easy. Computer scientist David Fuess is quoted as saying, "Google makes search look simple, but in fact, search is not simple, particularly when completeness is important" (Robb, 2007). Although everyone would prefer a "searching is simple" approach to research, individuals should be encouraged to see its complex qualities as well.

If general-purpose search engines offer a second message, it is that there should be no need to look for answers beyond the first results screen. Although no search engine overtly claims that all the best results are indeed found in the top ten, the notion is implied and certainly this expectation has taken hold in the minds of users. To be sure, that assumption is correct at times. Good resources that answer the search request may indeed be found at the top of the results list. The negative side of this message, however, is the "make-do" or "good-enough" attitude that begins to prevail about the top ten results. Gary Price, long an exponent of the Invisible Web, has begun to define anything beyond the top ten results as part of the Invisible Web because searchers are unwilling to explore beyond the first screen (Notess, 2006: 167). With many users, this reluctance has become a habit that may require persistence to overcome. The Invisible Web represents a great leap beyond general-purpose search engine results.

A final message that users absorb from general-purpose search engines may be called "one-stop shopping," the notion that one tool can serve to answer all questions and cover all subjects and situations. The Invisible Web does not have a one-tool solution; finding answers may often require using several kinds of tools. It may be hard to counter the appeal of "one-stop shopping," and it is always difficult to change habits, but there seems an obligation on the part of librarians and educators to try to draw people away from this one-dimensional approach to research. After all, what kind of world would it be if everyone only used Google's top ten results?

Thus, introducing students to the Invisible Web means countering these general-purpose search engine lessons, even though knowledge of search engine searching is a prerequisite. Fortunately, the object is not to replace general-purpose search engines but to show how Invisible Web resources complement search engine results. The Invisible Web can help close what Alex Salkever has called the "Google Gap—the difference between the growing perception that the site is omniscient and the fact that it isn't" (Salkever, 2003). The Invisible Web need not be put in a competitive situation with general-purpose search engines, although comparisons will ensue. The main message is that, when needed, richer resources are available that can solve research problems, and the best researchers know how to use them.

When and Where to Teach Use of the Invisible Web

The ideal scenario for teaching about the Invisible Web would be a whole class devoted to introducing its riches. Some circumstances may permit such classes, but the more likely situation will be far briefer opportunities that become available in conjunction with other instructional goals, such as a class on researching a specific topic. As explained in the following, the Invisible Web can be learned in stages. A number of concepts can be presented separately or in combination that contribute ideas to understanding the whole. Once the steps are identified, it is much easier to look for appropriate venues for presenting the information to students.

The next section of this chapter presents a series of concepts to incorporate in teaching about research that will help introduce the Invisible Web. These concepts are also mapped to the Association of College and Research Libraries (ACRL) *Information Literacy Competency Standards for Higher Education,* published in 2000 (see Appendix C for the complete text of these standards). Reference is also made to the American Association of School Librarians' *Standards for the 21st-Century Learner* (AASL, 2007).

STAGES FOR LEARNING ABOUT THE INVISIBLE WEB

This section is based on the premise that introducing the Invisible Web to students should and can take place in stages.

▶ The first stage is not about the Invisible Web but, rather, about the basics of searching the Web in general, starting with the surface Web and general-purpose search engines. Learning about the surface Web can also set the stage for a better understanding of the Invisible Web by creating an expectation for more and better search results.

▶ Once those expectations are in place, more explicit Stage Two discussions of the Invisible Web can follow.

▶ A third and final stage offers a more complete picture of Invisible Web searching.

The concepts suggested in this chapter may not deal with the whole Invisible Web package. It will rarely be possible or appropriate to introduce the Invisible Web fully at one time. A good beginning suggests that Web material exists beyond general-purpose search engine results. An important first step in setting the stage for the Invisible Web is to let people know how much information is not accessible through general-purpose search engines. Other important messages include search skills with new tools, the need to seek more specialized tools for specific problems, and issues of quality in search results. These messages expand horizons, as indeed does understanding the Invisible Web.

Each of the three stages is composed of concepts that in total create the bigger picture of the Invisible Web. The advantage of these concept messages is that they can be presented separately when needed or in response to situations that call for them. They can easily be incorporated into lesson plans. They may not need to be sequenced. They can be mixed and matched even across levels. Not everyone will need all of them to progress to the next stage of learning. These concepts can be adapted to fit many scenarios for presentation. Individuals can learn the material without feeling that they are being given a "lesson."

Introduction to the Invisible Web and growing understanding of it by users reflects progress toward making individuals competent in information use and as independent researchers. The ACRL *Information Literacy Competency Standards* offer a measured approach to information literacy with five basic structured and hierarchical standards. Tables 3-1 and 3-2 (see following sections) identify the ACRL Standards, Performance Indicators, and Outcomes that apply to each concept. The tables also reference the AASL *Standards for the 21st-Century Learner.* The AASL Standards are arranged differently from the ACRL Standards; they are organized by goals and are less hierarchical, although they support many of the same ideals.

Stage One Concepts: Web Searching Basics

Establishing basic ideas about Web searching makes possible deeper exploration that will lead students to the Invisible Web. The first concepts might include the following:

1. *Web searching skills.* As previously established in Chapter 2, many people do not use advanced general-purpose search engine features; many do not even do simple phrase searching with quotation marks. People who can use search engines more effectively will begin to see that better results are possible. As better searchers, they may build higher expectations for themselves and for their search results.
2. *Realistic expectations for Web searching.* Delivering the idea that general-purpose search engines are good for some kinds of questions but less effective for others is an important first step toward introducing the Invisible Web.
3. *Using more than one tool for research.* Multiple tools include databases, subscription databases, and library catalogs, all parts of the Invisible Web.
4. *Basic evaluation of resources.* This is a must for any information literacy effort. It is also important that people learn to look for better answers, not just "make do" or "good enough" answers. Basic steps here might include a review of domains, "About Us" statements, and currency. Many fine guides on the Web can help with evaluation instruction. One such guide, written by Susan Beck, is *The Good, the Bad, & the Ugly or, Why It's a Good Idea to Evaluate Web Sources* (Beck, 2008).
5. *How to adapt search phrasing when needed.* The skill of broadening or refining searches applies to general-purpose search engines but also suggests that steps need to be taken to get better results rather than simply settling for the first ten results of the first search attempt.
6. *It is all right to be dissatisfied with search results.* No rule promises that researchers get the best results the first time out. Research sometimes means experimenting with keywords and paraphrasing. Most important is to

recognize poor results and seek better ones. Those who do are on the road to becoming information literate.

7. *Subscription databases.* Available through schools, public libraries, and in academic settings, these databases are carefully selected to give students the kinds of resources they need. Students may initially see these databases as more difficult to use than general-purpose search engines, especially as compared to the simple Google search screen, but the databases are actually designed to make students' research much easier. Using the right tool can simplify and speed research, which is a welcome message to deliver to students at any time. Students cross over to the Invisible Web as soon as they learn how to access a subscription database.

8. *Using social networking sites for research.* Students will use these resources anyway, but they should be discussed in comparison with other tools that might prove more helpful. Comparing tools will help shape judgment about what constitutes good research.

9. *A first introduction to the Invisible Web.* Without a lengthy introduction at this stage, students should begin to hear about the existence of the Invisible Web and what it represents.

10. *General-purpose search engines promoted as tools, not solutions.*

11. *Where to go for help.* This basic message refers students to librarians and educators for further assistance. Closer analysis of these concepts shows that they suggest that it is permissible to feel dissatisfied at times with search engine results, introduce ideas about going beyond general-purpose search engines to other tools and choices, build awareness of the need to evaluate sources, and even introduce the Invisible Web in a very general way. These basic concepts actually achieve a great deal of progress toward understanding the Invisible Web and do much to further information literacy. Their effectiveness is demonstrated in Table 3-1, which groups Stage One concepts by instructional objective and then maps them to the ACRL *Information Literacy Competency Standards* and AASL Standards. The concepts have been grouped together into five categories: Search Engine Basics, Searching Tools, Evaluation of Information, Invisible Web Vocabulary, and Availability of Further Help.

As noted earlier, the ACRL Standards address information literacy in a "logical hierarchy" of competencies that includes *knowing* information needs and *accessing, evaluating,* and *using* information; some overlap occurs among certain aspects of the competencies. Performance indicators answer the question, "What do we want students to learn?" and outcomes answer the question, "How do we know that the student has learned?"

This review excludes ACRL Standard Five, which deals with the *ethical use* of information, a necessary discussion by itself. It also omits references to the AASL Standard 3, which deals with the same subject. It might be argued that students who have achieved a command of research skills, including Invisible Web

▶TABLE 3-1: Stage One Concepts Mapped to Information Literacy Standards		
A: Search Engine Basics		
Concepts	ACRL Standards	AASL Standards
1. Web searching skills. 2. Realistic expectations for Web searching. 5. Adapting search phrasing when needed. 6. It is all right to be dissatisfied with search results.	**Standard One:** Knowing the nature and extent of the information needed. Performance Indicator 1: Defining information need. *Outcome 1.C:* Explores general information sources to increase familiarity with the topic. Performance Indicator 3: Considering costs and benefits of the search. *Outcome 3.A:* Determines the availability of needed information and makes decisions on broadening the information seeking process beyond local resources. **Standard Two:** Accessing information. Performance Indicator 1: Selecting effective investigative methods. *Outcome 1.D:* Selects efficient and effective approaches for accessing the information needed from the investigative method or information retrieval system. Performance Indicator 4: Refining search strategy *Outcome 4.B:* Identifies gaps in the information retrieved and determines if the search strategy should be revised. *Outcome 4.C:* Repeats the search using the revised strategy as necessary. **Standard Three:** Evaluating information Performance Indicator 7: Determining need for query revision *Outcome 7.A:* Determines if original information need has been satisfied or if additional information is needed. *Outcome 7.B:* Reviews search strategy and incorporates additional concepts as necessary.	**Standard One:** Inquire, think critically, and gain knowledge. 1.1.4: Find, evaluate, and select appropriate sources to answer questions. 1.2.5: Demonstrate adaptability by changing the inquiry focus, questions, resources, or strategies when necessary to achieve success. **Standard Two:** Draw conclusions, make informed decisions, apply knowledge to new situations, and create new knowledge. 2.4.1: Determine how to act on information (accept, reject, modify).

Continued

▶TABLE 3-1 *Continued*		
B: Searching Tools		
Concepts	ACRL Standards	AASL Standards
1. Realistic expectations for Web searching. 2. Idea of using more than one tool to search. 7. Subscription databases. 8. Using social networking sites for research. 10. General-purpose search engines as tools, not solutions.	**Standard Two:** Accessing information. Performance Indicator 1: Selecting effective investigative methods. *Outcome 1.C:* Investigates the scope, content, and organization of information retrieval systems. Performance Indicator 2: Implementing effective search strategies. *Outcome 2.E:* Implements the search strategy in various information retrieval systems using different user interfaces and search engines. Performance Indicator 3: Retrieving information using a variety of sources and methods. *Outcome 3.C:* Uses specialized online or in person services available at the institution to retrieve information needed. Performance Indicator 4: Refining search strategy. *Outcome 4.A:* Assesses the quantity, quality, and relevance of the search results to determine whether alternative information retrieval systems or investigative methods should be utilized. **Standard Three:** Evaluating information. Performance Indicator 7: Determining need for query revision. *Outcome 7.C:* Reviews information retrieval sources used and expands to include others as needed.	**Standard One:** Inquire, think critically, and gain knowledge. 1.2.3: Demonstrate creativity by using multiple resources and formats. **Standard Two:** Draw conclusions, make informed decisions, apply knowledge to new situations, and create new knowledge. 2.4.1: Determine how to act on information (accept, reject, modify). **Standard Four:** Pursue personal and aesthetic growth. 4.1.7: Use social networks and information tools to gather and share information. 4.3.2: Recognize that resources are created for a variety of purposes.

Continued

▷ TABLE 3-1 *Continued*		
C: Evaluation of Information		
Concepts	ACRL Standards	AASL Standards

3. Basic steps for evaluation of resources.
6. It is all right to be dissatisfied with search results.
	Standard Two: Accessing information.
	Performance Indicator 1:
	  Selecting effective investigative methods.
	Outcome 1.C: Investigates the scope, content, and organization of information retrieval systems.
	Performance Indicator 4:
	  Refining search strategy.
	Outcome 4.A: Assesses the quantity, quality, and relevance of the search results to determine whether alternative information retrieval systems or investigative methods should be utilized.
	Standard Three: Evaluating information.
	Performance Indicator 2:
	  Articulating and applying evaluation criteria.
	Outcome 2.A: Examines and compares information from various sources in order to evaluate reliability, validity, accuracy, authority, timeliness, and point of view or bias.
	Performance Indicator 4:
	  Comparing new knowledge to old to determine value.
	Outcome 4.E: Determines probable accuracy by questioning the source of the data, the limitations of the information gathering tools or strategies, and the reasonableness of the conclusions.
		Standard One: Inquire, think critically, and gain knowledge.
		1.1.4: Find, evaluate, and select appropriate sources to answer questions.
		1.1.5: Evaluate information found in selected sources on the basis of accuracy, validity, appropriateness for needs, importance, and social and cultural context.
		1.2.4: Maintain a critical stance by questioning the validity and accuracy of all information.
		1.2.6: Display emotional resilience by persisting in information searching despite challenges.

Continued

▶TABLE 3-1 *Continued*		
D: Invisible Web Vocabulary		
Concepts	**ACRL Standards**	**AASL Standards**
9. Introduce the Invisible Web and what it represents.	**Standard One:** Knowing the nature and extent of the information needed. <u>Performance Indicator 2</u>: Identifying information types and formats. *Outcome 2.B:* Recognizes that knowledge can be organized into disciplines that influence the way information is accessed.	**Standard Two:** Draw conclusions, make informed decisions, apply knowledge to new situations, and create new knowledge. 2.4.3: Recognize new knowledge and understanding. **Standard Four:** Pursue personal and aesthetic growth. 4.3.2: Recognize that resources are created for a variety of purposes.
E: Availability of Further Help		
Concepts	**ACRL Standards**	**AASL Standards**
11. Teaching where to go for help.	**Standard Two:** Accessing information. <u>Performance Indicator 3</u>: Retrieving information using a variety of sources and methods. *Outcome 3.C:* Uses specialized online or in person services available at the institution to retrieve information needed. **Standard Three:** Evaluating information. <u>Performance Indicator 6</u>: Validating information with others. *Outcome 6.C:* Seeks expert opinion through a variety of mechanisms.	**Standard One:** Inquire, think critically, and gain knowledge. 1.4.2: Use interaction with and feedback from teachers and peers to guide own inquiry process. 1.4.4: Seek appropriate help when it is needed.

Source: ACRL Standards are excerpted from *Information Literacy Competency Standards* and reprinted with permission of the Association of College and Research Libraries, American Library Association. AASL Standards are excerpted from *Standards for the 21st-Century Learner* by the American Association of School Librarians, a division of the American Library Association, copyright © 2007 American Library Association. Available for download at www.ala.org/aasl/standards. Reprinted with permission.

resources, might be less inclined to plagiarize, but that statement might be more wishful thinking than reality. A definite need exists for discussion about the ethical use of information with students. That discussion is part of information literacy but does not address the concerns of this chapter, which are about building skills in using the Invisible Web.

Sample Assignment

A sample research assignment illustrates how these concepts could be introduced in a specific situation. Let us suppose that students have been asked to do their first research assignment for a class on economics and have been given the topic of "microfinance" to explore. The teacher of such a class will discuss the expectations for this research project. It would be easy to talk about general searching as a starting point, recognizing that most students will turn first to general-purpose search engines such as Google and Yahoo!. The teacher can introduce as part of the assignment some basic expectations such as the need for students to use more than one search tool. The teacher may also cover some basic skills in evaluating search results to instill some sense of choosing appropriate materials for the report. The teacher may also mention some specific subscription databases that are available to the students, and this opportunity can provide an introduction to the Invisible Web. (See Chapter 5 for a more in-depth analysis of a research case study.)

Even in this basic discussion of research, several concepts have been covered. They begin setting in place the building blocks needed to appreciate Invisible Web resources. Students who succeed at this research level are ready for more demanding assignments.

Stage Two Concepts: Presenting the Invisible Web

The next phase introduces the Invisible Web more specifically. Having gained some experience upon which to base judgments, students are ready to advance. The next concepts might include the following:

1. *High expectations.* Messages about raising expectations counter a lazy student attitude that wants only to go to a general-purpose search engine, find, and use only the first results screen. Students should require more from themselves and their information tools when they select sources to use for research projects. It can also establish the expectation that some research is complex and time-consuming.

2. *Multiple search tools.* The expectation at this stage is that students are refining their searches on a regular basis and are open to the notion that more than one research tool may be needed and helpful. This discussion can be expanded to introduce directories, specialized search engines, and specialized databases as well as the idea that these resources represent Invisible Web materials.

3. *Search engines can help find Invisible Web tools.* Google, Yahoo! and other general-purpose search engines can be used to find directories, specialized databases, specialized search engines, and the like. Search engines can locate Invisible Web tools; they just cannot retrieve information from them. This approach is called "split level searching. The first level locates the database site; the second level searches the database" (Cohen, 2005: 10).

4. *Size of Invisible Web compared with size of surface Web* (see Chapter 7 for more detailed information about the size of the Invisible Web).

5. *Characteristics of Invisible Web resources.*

6. *Peer review and other advanced indicators of authority.*

7. *Formats that are not well represented by general-purpose search engines and the tools that can help locate them.* These resources are often part of the Invisible Web.

8. *Research vocabulary or, as some might call it, library vocabulary.* This vocabulary may include subjects that range from Boolean operators to the distinctions between directories, catalogs, databases, etc.

9. *Student-created research journals in which they explain their research process and choices.* Such journals encourage reflection on the research process, but may be possible only in class settings where research is assigned and given a lot of attention.

10. *In-depth and specialized searching.* Techniques include vertical searching, searching deeply within individual Web sites, domain-specific searching, and searching in specific subject areas.

11. *Niche search engines* (see Chapter 6 for examples of niche tools).

12. *Creation of bookmarks of favorite tools for return use.* These favorites or "mylibraries" should include a mixture of general-purpose search engines and Invisible Web resources.

13. *Help.* Remind students frequently of where they can seek help with research projects.

This second range of concepts addresses the Invisible Web directly with sections on its characteristics and how to use it. Stage Two concepts also advance general search ability to more complex skill levels. The concepts can definitely be realigned and used as seems best for the situation in a practical mix-and-match approach. That also applies to intermixing Stage One and Stage Two concepts.

Table 3-2 groups Stage Two concepts and maps them to the ACRL and AASL Standards.

Sample Assignment

Let us suppose that the same students from our earlier example are given another research assignment about microfinance, only this time they must deal with the specific topic of "microcredit." In preparing for this research assignment their teacher may want to include some discussion about using more specialized search tools, perhaps suggesting databases and special search engines that deal with the topic well. The teacher might even demonstrate how to find these specialized tools using Google. It might be a good opportunity to reference the Invisible Web directly by including its resources for consideration. This discussion sets higher expectations for the students' resources.

As this lesson continues, it should also include ways of evaluating resources, defining the concept of peer-reviewed materials and other measures of reliability and bias. Finally, any preparation for research should also include mention of where to find further help. (See Chapter 5 for a more in-depth analysis of a research case study.)

These few steps have incorporated several concepts and built on the students' previous experience to develop more research skills.

▶TABLE 3-2: Stage Two Concepts Mapped to Information Literacy Standards		
A: Using Multiple Resources		
Concepts	ACRL Standards	AASL Standards
1. High expectations. 2. Multiple search tools. 3. Search engines used to find Invisible Web tools. 6. Formats that are not well represented by general-purpose search engines and the tools that can help locate them. 7. Research vocabulary. 10. In-depth and specialized searching 11. Specialized niche search engines.	**Standard One:** Knowing the nature and extent of the information needed. Performance Indicator 2: Identifying information types and formats. *Outcome 2.B:* Recognizes that knowledge can be organized into disciplines that influence the way information is accessed. **Standard Two:** Accessing information. Performance Indicator 1: Selecting effective investigative methods. *Outcome 1.C:* Investigates the scope, content, and organization of information retrieval systems. Performance Indicator 2: Implementing effective search strategies. *Outcome 2.E:* Implements the search strategy in various information retrieval systems using different user interfaces and search engines. Performance Indicator 4: Refining search strategy. *Outcome 4.A:* Assesses the quantity, quality, and relevance of the search results to determine whether alternative information retrieval systems or investigative methods should be utilized. **Standard Three:** Evaluating information. Performance indicator 7: Determining need for query revision. *Outcome 7.C:* Reviews information retrieval sources used and expands to include others as needed.	**Standard One:** Inquire, think critically, and gain knowledge. 1.2.3: Demonstrate creativity by using multiple resources and formats. 1.2.6: Display emotional resilience by persisting in information searching despite challenges. 1.4.3: Monitor gathered information, and assess for gaps or weaknesses. **Standard Two:** Draw conclusions, make informed decisions, apply knowledge to new situations, and create new knowledge. 2.2.1: Demonstrate flexibility in the use of resources by adapting information strategies to each specific resource and by seeking additional resources when clear conclusions cannot be drawn. 2.4.2: Reflect on systematic process, and assess for completeness of investigation. **Standard Four:** Pursue personal and aesthetic growth. 4.3.2: Recognize that resources are created for a variety of purposes.

Continued

▶ TABLE 3-2 *Continued*		
B: Evaluation of Information		
Concepts	ACRL Standards	AASL Standards
1. High expectations. 1. Peer review and other advanced indicators of authority.	**Standard One:** Knowing the nature and extent of information needed. Performance Indicator 2: Identifying information types and formats. *Outcome 2.D:* Identifies the purpose and audience of potential resources. **Standard Two:** Accessing information. Performance Indicator 1: Selecting effective investigative methods. *Outcome 1.C:* Investigates the scope, content, and organization of information retrieval systems. Performance Indicator 2: Implementing effective search strategies. *Outcome 2.E:* Implements the search strategy in various information retrieval systems using different user interfaces and search engines. Performance Indicator 4: Refining search strategy. *Outcome 4.A:* Assesses the quantity, quality, and relevance of the search results to determine whether alternative information retrieval systems or investigative methods should be utilized. **Standard Three:** Evaluating information. Performance Indicator 2: Articulating and applying evaluation criteria. *Outcome 2.A:* Examines and compares information from various sources in order to evaluate reliability, validity, accuracy, authority, timeliness, and point of view or bias. Performance Indicator 4: Comparing new knowledge to old to determine value. *Outcome 4.A:* Determines whether information satisfies the research or other information need. *Outcome 4.E:* Determines probable accuracy by questioning the source of the data, the limitations of the information gathering tools or strategies, and the reasonableness of the conclusions.	**Standard One:** Inquire, think critically, and gain knowledge. 1.1.8: Demonstrate mastery of technology tools for accessing information and pursuing inquiry. 1.2.2: Demonstrate confidence and self-direction by making independent choices in the selection of resources and information. 1.2.4: Maintain a critical stance by questioning the validity and accuracy of all information. **Standard Two:** Draw conclusions, make informed decisions, apply knowledge to new situations, and create new knowledge. 2.4.2: Reflect on systematic process, and assess for completeness of investigation. **Standard Four:** Pursue personal and aesthetic growth. 4.3.2: Recognize that resources are created for a variety of purposes.

Continued

▷ **TABLE 3-2** *Continued*		
C: Advanced Techniques		
Concepts	ACRL Standards	AASL Standards
2. Introducing multiple search tools. 3. Using search engines to locate Invisible Web tools. 7. Introducing formats that are not well represented by general-purpose search engines and the tools that can help locate them. 9. Encouraging students to create research journals in which they explain their research process and choices. 12. Encouraging the creation of bookmarks of favorite tools for return use. 13. Reminding people frequently of where they can still seek help with research projects.	**Standard One:** Knowing the nature and extent of the information needed. Performance Indicator 1: Defining the information need. *Outcome 1.D:* Defines or modifies the information need to achieve a manageable focus. Performance Indicator 2: Identifying information types and formats. *Outcome 2.B:* Recognizes that knowledge can be organized into disciplines that influence the way information is accessed. *Outcome 2.C:* Identifies the value and differences of potential resources in a variety of formats. **Standard Two:** Accessing information. Performance Indicator 2: Implementing effective search strategies. *Outcome 2.E:* Implements the search strategy in various information retrieval systems using different user interfaces and search engines. Performance Indicator 3: Retrieving information using a variety of sources and methods. *Outcome 3.A:* Uses various search systems to retrieve information in a variety of formats. *Outcome 3.C:* Uses specialized online or in person service available at the institution to retrieve information needed. **Standard Two:** Accessing information. Performance Indicator 4: Refining search strategy. *Outcome 4.B:* Identifies gaps in the information retrieved and determines if the search strategy should be revised. *Outcome 4.C:* Repeats the search using the revised strategy as necessary. **Standard Three:** Evaluating information. Performance Indicator 4: Comparing new knowledge to old to determine value. *Outcome 4.A:* Determines whether information satisfies the research or other information need.	**Standard One:** Inquire, think critically, and gain knowledge. 1.1.4: Find, evaluate, and select appropriate sources to answer questions. 1.1.6: Read, view, and listen for information presented in any format (e.g., textual, visual, media, digital) in order to make inferences and gather meaning. 1.2.2: Demonstrate confidence and self-direction by making independent choices in the selection of resources and information. 1.2.3: Demonstrate creativity by using multiple resources and formats. 1.4.2: Use interaction with and feedback from teachers and peers to guide own inquiry process. 1.4.3: Monitor gathered information, and assess for gaps or weaknesses. 1.4.4: Seek appropriate help when it is needed. **Standard Four:** Pursue personal and aesthetic growth. 4.2.1: Display curiosity by pursuing interests through multiple resources.

Continued

▶TABLE 3-2 *Continued*		
D: Using Invisible Web Resources		
Concepts	ACRL Standards	AASL Standards
4. Teaching the size of the Invisible Web compared with the surface Web. 5. Teaching the characteristics of Invisible Web resources.	**Standard One:** Knowing the nature and extent of the information needed. Performance Indicator 2: Identifying information types and formats. *Outcome 2.C:* Identifies the value and differences of potential resources in a variety of formats. **Standard Two:** Accessing information. Performance Indicator 3: Retrieving information using a variety of sources and methods. *Outcome 3.A:* Uses various search systems to retrieve information in a variety of formats.	**Standard One:** Inquire, think critically, and gain knowledge. 1.1.8: Demonstrate mastery of technology tools for accessing information and pursuing inquiry. 1.2.2: Demonstrate confidence and self-direction by making independent choices in the selection of resources and information. 1.2.3: Demonstrate creativity by using multiple resources and formats. **Standard Two:** Draw conclusions, make informed decisions, apply knowledge to new situations, and create new knowledge. 2.4.2: Reflect on systematic process, and assess for completeness of investigation. **Standard Four:** Pursue personal and aesthetic growth. 4.2.1: Display curiosity by pursuing interests through multiple resources.

Source: ACRL Standards are excerpted from *Information Literacy Competency Standards* and reprinted with permission of the Association of College and Research Libraries, American Library Association. AASL Standards are excerpted from *Standards for the 21st-Century Learner* by the American Association of School Librarians, a division of the American Library Association, copyright © 2007 American Library Association. Available for download at www.ala.org/aasl/standards. Reprinted with permission.

Stage Three Concepts: The Riches of the Invisible Web

Stage One and Stage Two concepts accomplish much toward making students better searchers. Students may stay on these levels as long as needed. When they have absorbed most or all of the practices encouraged in Stages One and Two, they will recognize the Invisible Web as a collection of valuable resources to be used when and if needed. Stage Three concepts build on that understanding and are exclusively about the Invisible Web. They include the following:

1. General-purpose search engine findings are supplemented regularly with searches that include Invisible Web tools. These resources can be used when search engines do not provide the desired results. Roy Tennant describes this process as "people waking up to the fact that the lowest common denominator searching is fine for some things but not for others" (Storey, 2007: 7).

2. Invisible Web resources provide specialized tools for subject research in the expectation that student research output ought to demonstrate more sophistication and advanced levels as they progress through higher education.
3. Use appropriate tools for upper level studies and research.
4. Use professional tools and sites appropriate for specialized fields of study and subject specialization that can carry over for individuals as they go out to work in their chosen fields and occupations. Students with knowledge of these Invisible Web resources will have a competitive edge over their peers about information and research in their chosen careers.

The ACRL and AASL Standards do not need referencing at this point.

Students at Stage Three know what the Invisible Web is and have a sense that it should be part of their research process. They make informed decisions about their research needs. They recognize that searching does not end with general-purpose search engines, and that other tools are available to find more and richer resources. They may use Invisible Web resources for more than classroom and academic needs and continue to explore the Web for good resources. They can explain the Invisible Web to their friends and guide others to its use. As suggested by the previous analysis, the instructional objectives of all the concepts form information literacy skills and advance information literacy competencies.

OPPORTUNITIES FOR INVISIBLE WEB INSTRUCTION

Although it is easy to assume that students already know a lot about the World Wide Web, it is clear from studies of student search practices (see Chapter 2) that guidance from teachers and librarians can help them become more successful Web researchers. Teachers and librarians must help students form the bigger picture from all of the bits and pieces. Many who have allowed general-purpose search engines to be their sole research teacher never form a complete picture of the Web information world.

Material on a library Web site or a teacher's Web page or in a courseware link can demonstrate points to be made. Librarians can create online guides or tutorials to help classroom instruction or to be used to reinforce lessons later. Teachers can maintain their own lists of links in courseware or they can collaborate with librarians or link to the many guides available on the Web.

Introducing the Invisible Web in Reference Work

The Reference Desk

As described by Christina M. Desai and Stephanie J. Graves (2008), reference work can offer "the teachable moment" but it does not always offer much time to develop research building blocks. Academic and school reference librarians give attention to showing and explaining research choices. They also give attention to the concept of evaluating resources. Ideally, they teach the user to find results and make information decisions. Assessing the expertise of the user always plays an important role in satisfying the user's needs and also in recognizing opportunities to introduce advanced searching skills such as the Invisible Web.

Reference desks get both "ready reference," quickly answered questions, and in-depth research questions. Some in both categories can be answered quickly and do not require lengthy, lesson-based exchanges. The surface Web may be a good place to start for both. Often, students may need to explore a subject broadly as the first phase of a research assignment, leaving consideration of more diverse choices to an appropriate later time as they refine their searches.

For more in-depth research, many libraries have the advantage of offering subscription databases, an ideal collection of resources for their community of users. Subscription databases represent two characteristics of the Invisible Web very clearly: They are databases and, as such, require that users fill out an individualized search request form. They are restricted to community members who must identify themselves as part of that community (see Chapter 6 for examples). However, it does not follow that it is always appropriate to introduce these tools and their Invisible Web traits at the reference desk. The opportunity must be dictated by the user, the user's knowledge of research, and whether the research building blocks are in place for the user to understand the concepts. There may be time, however, to present concepts that flow naturally from a discussion of research choices. Such concepts can be especially timely when the student is already dissatisfied with results retrieved using general-purpose search engines. That dissatisfaction is an open invitation for the reference librarian to begin to introduce Invisible Web concepts. In-depth questions also create an easy situation within which to introduce the Invisible Web, if not overtly, by suggesting some of its resources specifically.

Other Reference Venues

Virtual reference has all the constraints of ready reference and the added difficulty of communicating without seeing a person and how she or he is reacting to the material being shown. Success may also depend on technology skills.

Advisory reference, however, gives students a chance to make an appointment for a research consultation and speak with a librarian at length and may offer more opportunities to introduce Invisible Web resources when appropriate.

Introducing the Invisible Web in the One-shot Instruction Period

Many academic and school libraries give one-hour or one-session classes designed to provide their students with a basic understanding of library resources. Public libraries often provide this kind of introduction/instruction workshop as well, either in collaboration with a school program or as part of their general-purpose services to users. In most of these classes there is no time to create a whole instructional session around the Invisible Web. Working with the instructor for a particular course also means adapting the class presentation to the course syllabus.

Another question goes back to student needs. Is the class intended for students who are at an early stage in their college studies? Do the students have much sense of or experience with the research process? Do they have a good basic understanding about information resources? Will part of the time be spent on traditional library resources as well as the Web realm? If the class is voluntary, there may be a great unevenness in the participants' understanding of research and the Web world of information. If the students know little about searching the Web, then dividing the Web into the surface and Invisible Webs will not make much sense.

So, what are the opportunities presented by these one-shot programs? While it will probably not be possible to do much exploration of the Invisible Web, it may be possible to begin a class with some concept. For instance, ask students what general-purpose search engines they use and then how much of the Web they believe that their choice searches. They may be surprised that their search engine of choice tracks less than 20 percent of the resources available to them (Bergman, 2001). This realization can lead to the introduction of the idea that many search tools can provide help. Perhaps this idea can be taken one step further to suggest that they always consider using more than one tool when they have research to complete. Just these few brief steps help create the impression that the information world is much larger than Google, Yahoo!, or Live Search. Of course, at this point it would be nice to be able to talk about the Invisible Web, but it is not necessary. If the library Web site has a guide or tutorial about the Invisible Web, this might be the appropriate moment to mention it.

Library classes often introduce users to subscription databases, and it is possible to include an explanation of their role in the Invisible Web. Subscription electronic resources come in many formats, but those that are databases can also introduce the importance of databases to the Invisible Web.

Introducing the Invisible Web in Credit Courses

A credit-bearing course in information literacy is the ideal scenario within which to tackle the Invisible Web. The Invisible Web easily forms part of the syllabus in such a course, and students can benefit from all of the building-block concepts that can be set in place before it is introduced. The Invisible Web lesson can be much more extensive, a part of regular discussions about the World Wide Web, and reinforced by activities, assignments and follow-up. Especially effective are comparisons of Invisible Web tools and how they work with surface Web tools. Many tools can be explored, such as catalogs, directories, and databases, and the point at which they cross over into the Invisible Web can be analyzed. (See Chapter 6 for examples of these kinds of tools.) A credit-bearing class offers more time to develop every idea associated with the Invisible Web.

Invisible Web content can also form part of credit-bearing courses that are not information literacy classes as such but are subject- or discipline-specific. Subject specialization often entails the use of more specialized resources. Introducing subject-oriented databases and professional Web sites, for instance, brings students closer to, if not actually within, the Invisible Web. Students can be expected to be familiar with the resources that are important to their subject specialization, and their choices of research tools should reflect growing sophistication. In addition, students can undertake vertical searching of Web sites, navigating them and taking away more than just the surface information. The instructor can have informative guides and links ready to demonstrate.

Introducing the Invisible Web with Course Management Systems

In today's classroom, professors are likely to use course management systems, such as Blackboard, which provide an online component to the course. Instructors can post syllabi, assignments, and external links and ask students to post messages on a discussion board. All of these features lend themselves to introducing the Invisible Web, whether in preparation for a research paper or for other research-based assignments.

An obvious step is for the instructor to link students to the library's homepage as an aid to research. Such a link also establishes a relationship between the course content and the library and supports the message that the instructor wants students to use more than general-purpose search engines. A teacher can take an additional step and provide links to Web resources, some of which would be considered part of the Invisible Web; an example is the Librarian's Internet Index (http://www.lii.org) (see Chapter 6 for more in-depth information). Instructors can also work with librarians on campus and create vetted lists of links relating to class research topics. Blackboard, for example, offers an "External Links" tab for easy placement of these resources. Links can also be created to guides and tutorials that support Invisible Web instruction.

Many librarians get the opportunity to work as research consultants for courses and Blackboard discussion boards and can act as mentors, encouraging use of wider selections of resources that include Invisible Web materials. Any increase in the level of visibility for Invisible Web resources contributes to the increased use of these rich, underutilized resources.

Other Opportunities for Introducing the Invisible Web

Librarians and classroom instructors can look for opportunities to introduce the Invisible Web in formal and informal workshops for faculty and students. Some schools have student research clubs or academies that bear exploration. A growing number of schools are offering their students electronic portfolios or ePortfolios, which give students an online environment in which to deposit work, manage their assignments, and reflect on learning. Librarians and instructors should explore ways to connect with their school's ePortfolio projects. Other venues for promoting the Invisible Web include "shop talk" about research tools among faculty colleagues and articles in campus publications.

SUMMARY

This chapter started with the premise that it takes preparatory steps to build an understanding of the Invisible Web and its part in the Web information world. Although the Invisible Web exists as an extension of the resources found by general-purpose search engines, it does not supplant them; rather, it complements them and offers an opportunity to take a more complete approach to research when needed. Introducing students to the Invisible Web can take place on many different levels and in many situations.

REFERENCES

American Association of School Librarians. 2007. *Standards for the 21st-Century Learner.* Available: www.ala.org/ala/mgrps/divs/aasl/aaslproftools/learningstandards/AASL_ Learning_Standards_2007.pdf (accessed December 6, 2008).

Association of College and Research Libraries. 2000. *Information Literacy Competency Standards for Higher Education.* Available: www.ala.org/ala/acrl/acrlstandards/ informationliteracycompetency. htm#ilhedcfm (accessed December 6, 2008).

Beck, Susan E. 2008. *The Good, the Bad, and the Ugly or, Why It's a Good Idea to Evaluate Web Sources.* Las Cruces, NM: New Mexico State University Library. Available: http://lib.nmsu.edu/ instruction/eval.html (accessed October 3, 2008).

Bergman, Michael K. 2001. "The deep Web: Surfacing hidden value." White paper. BrightPlanet. Available: www.brightplanet.com/images/stories/pdf/deepwebwhitepaper. pdf (accessed October 3, 2008).

Cohen, Laura B. 2005. "Finding scholarly content on the Web: From Google to RSS feeds." *Choice* 42 (Special issue): 7–8, 10, 12–17.

Desai, Christina M., and Stephanie J. Graves. 2008. "Cyberspace or face-to-face: The teachable moment and changing reference mediums." *Reference and User Services Quarterly* 47, no.3: 252–255.

Martin, Pamela. 2006. "Google as teacher: Everything your students know they learned from searching Google." *College & Research Libraries News* 67, no.2: 100–101.

Notess, Greg R. 2006. *Teaching Web Search Skills: Techniques and Strategies of Top Trainers.* Medford, NJ: Information Today.

Robb, Drew. 2007. "Exploring the deep web." *Government Computer News* 3 (June), no.4. Available: www.gcn.com/print/26_13/44415-1.html (accessed October 3, 2008).

Salkever, Alex. 2003. "The Web, according to Google." *Business Week Online* 10, no.23 (June). Available: www.businessweek.com/technology/content/jun2003/tc20030610_2810_tc104.htm (accessed October 3, 2008).

Storey, Tom. 2007. "Search for tomorrow: Preparing for a new age in information gathering." *NextSpace* 1, no.6: 7. Available: www.oclc.org/nextspace/006/default.htm (accessed October 3, 2008).

►4

FURTHER EXPLORATION
OF THE INVISIBLE WEB

INTRODUCTION

So far, arguments have been made that more people should know about Invisible Web resources and that, when research is needed, more people should make it part of their regular reference toolkit. This leads to some obvious questions: Where do I find the Invisible Web? When do I know that I am using it? The truth is that most Invisible Web resources are not labeled as such and the Web world is always changing so that label may go out of date quickly. The fluidity of Invisible Web resources begs the question: How can anyone ever really know them when they see them? The answer would be much easier if the Invisible Web had a one-tool solution like the surface Web, but it does not. That complexity alone may be enough to send people back to their favorite general-purpose search engines and forget about the whole thing.

This chapter suggests some activities that can help anyone learn more about the Invisible Web. The concrete activities that follow will inform about the Web world of information, suggest the Invisible Web's place in it, and help people know when they are touching it. None of these activities will require more than access to the Web and some time and effort. The activities can be used by individuals or as group projects and may help educators, librarians, and students alike. As in Chapter 3, the suggested activities are aligned with the first three ALA *Information Literacy Competency Standards* objectives for those who may want to use these activities with students by incorporating them into their lesson plans. They are, briefly stated, "To Know," "To Access," and "To Evaluate." "To Use," which is the fourth ALA Standard, is presumed to be the outcome of all of the previous chapters of the book.

The first activity, "To Know," is intended to help individuals learn more about the Invisible Web by seeing how it is viewed and valued by others. This activity looks at news items that help tell the story of ongoing interest in the Invisible Web. These news items include new product announcements, new proposals for technical solutions, and general articles about the Invisible Web, many initiated by people who have discovered it for themselves. A lot of the news concerning Invisible Web developments takes place below the surface for most people. Announcements for new products to solve Invisible Web access problems seem intended for special audiences and not for general consumption. Therefore, to learn more about the Invisible Web, one may need to go to where people who are actively pursuing it are talking about it.

The "To Access" activity explores several steps that show how Invisible Web resources can be identified. This book includes a chapter that reviews tools for searching the Invisible Web (see Chapter 6). This activity concentrates on identification of, rather than on searching with, the tools. It may help answer these questions: How do I know when I have crossed over into Invisible Web resources? How many clicks down are needed to find it?

The "To Evaluate" activity is similar to the comparison of resources made in Chapter 3. It is based on concept mapping but, in this case, involves results mapping. Comparing results found by different research tools is still the best way to demonstrate the need to use more than one resource. It lends itself to any information literacy instruction. Comparisons may also give students the idea that reflecting on the tool they are using and the results they are getting is a good idea. The activity will map the results from a specialized search tool and see how they compare with general-purpose search engine results.

The authors hope that these activities complete the picture already made about the Invisible Web in previous chapters. Sometimes activities are more illustrative than straight text discussions and can help users get a live feel for the topic.

ACTIVITY 1: TO KNOW

Objective

The objective of this activity is to learn about the Invisible Web from what others have to say. One way to place a value on the Invisible Web is to learn the value that others place on it. Searching about the Invisible Web in databases and on the open Web is certainly a good way to learn about it, but that approach does not give a sense of any ongoing development nor does it identify where the current interest lies. The goal of this activity is to put a face on the interest that the Invisible Web generates.

Setup

All that is needed for this activity is to set up a Google Alert for the terms "Invisible Web," "Deep Web," and perhaps "Hidden Web." "Invisible Web" and "Deep

Web" are often used. The Invisible Web has also been called the "Hidden Web," but that term may also bring up material that relates to Web security issues. So, when using "Hidden Web," be prepared to review the material carefully for aspects of the information world that relate to the search.

It may seem ironic that, after stressing the limitations of general-purpose search engines like Google, we should use their alerting system. This is just another example of how the visible and Invisible Web connect and represent two aspects of one Web information world. Google Alerts are easily set up. (Go to this URL for further information: www.google.com/alerts.) Once the alerts start coming in, and they come once a week, the next step is to chart the postings and categorize them. It is best to look at a period of time, such as a month or two, to get a diverse body of material to review. The results will probably fall into some basic categories. For instance, it is common to see an information company announcing a new search engine or product that uncovers Invisible Web content. These new products may not become widely known because they target either specialized areas of information or specific users, such as those in the business world. Many may also be fee-based. Many are not intended to compete on the level of Google and other general-purpose search engines. Some may be new attempts that will fail due to lack of support.

Some Google Alerts may produce articles that introduce new concepts into the discussion. For instance, recent topics have included vertical searching and semantic approaches to Invisible Web access issues. They discuss new ideas and demonstrate new attempts to reach more Invisible Web content. To the extent that the Invisible Web poses a technical challenge, new theories and new technical approaches will attempt answers. Some articles will be general introductions to the Invisible Web. Some may come from individuals who are discovering the Invisible Web for the first time and are posting the information to a blog to share it with others. Articles are also still being written by librarians and teachers to further the discussions about the Invisible Web in the education world. Many serve as general introductions to the subject. In fact, only these introductory articles may be intended for general users. Company announcements target the business world and may come from trade and business news sites. Articles dealing with technical solutions or theories are intended for the information industry. All of these search results tell us something about the Invisible Web and why it remains important, even if not widely discussed. The exercise of charting and categorizing these Invisible Web materials can help create an image of the Invisible Web for others. It can also lead to discussions of vocabulary, theories of solving technical problems, and the evaluation of new products and what they offer the researcher. Seeing the diversity of products presented can be an education in itself to those who seldom go beyond the realm of Google and Yahoo!

Table 4-1 shows the charted results of Google Alerts using the three terms "Invisible Web," "Deep Web," and "Hidden Web" taken over the period from

▶ **TABLE 4-1: Google Alerts for "Deep Web," "Invisible Web," and "Hidden Web" for January and February 2007**

Date	Reference	Found Under	Category
1/8	Source: LinuxWorld.com.au URL: www.linuxworld.com.au/index.php/id; 　1925475684;fp;4;fpid;4 Title: "Mining the Deep Web: Search Strategies that Work" Author: Lee Ratzan Type of Material: Article dated 12/28/2006	Invisible Web	Introduction/ Guide
1/8	Source: bigmouthmedia—Industry News 1/8/07 URL: www.bigmouthmedia.com/live/articles/real-time- 　search-engine-nets-6-million-in-priva.asp/3400/ Title: "Real-Time Search Engine Nets $6 Million in Private 　Funding" Type of material: Article on ChaCha	Invisible Web	New Product announcement ChaCha Added value: Vocabulary: real time searching
1/8	Source: RMP301b2 URL: http://rmp301b2.blogspot.com/2007/01/deep- 　web-accessing-hidden-information.html Title: "The Deep Web: Accessing 'Hidden' Information on 　the Web" Author: Ansuya H. Type of material: Blog posting (no longer traceable)	Invisible Web	Introduction/ Guide
1/16	Source: Octora URL: http://www.octora.com Title: "Octora—RSS Feed Search Engines" Type of material: Search engine Web site. Search Engine offers a "Deep Search" option tab. (Originally learned from a blog posting that is no longer traceable.)	Deep Web	Product information Added value: RSS feeds
1/29	Source: WebKnowHow News URL: www.webknowhow.net/news/news/ 　070123ReportLinker.html Title: "ReportLinker, the Market Research Engine, Surpasses 　10,000 Beta Testers in 3 Weeks" Type of material: Article. "ReportLinker is the first 　professional search engine which allows users to access 　free market reports available on the deep web, also 　called invisible web."	Invisible Web	New product announcement Added value: Market research reports Fee based
1/29	Source: Forbes.com URL: www.forbes.com/business/2007/01/23/search- 　people-web-tech-cx_rr_0124search.html Title: "Snoop.com" Author: Rachel Rosmarin Type of material: Article. It mentions hidden Invisible Web 　content and that Google comes up short.	Invisible Web	Company announcement

Continued

▶TABLE 4-1 *Continued*			
Date	Reference	Found Under	Category
1/29	Source: Web Blog—Invisible URL: http://invisible.directtalks.org/2007/01/ what-is-invisible-web-and-how-dowhat.html (No longer accessible) Title: "What is the Invisible Web?" Type of material: Guide	Invisible Web	Introduction/ Guide
1/30	Source: Environment News Service URL: www.ens-newswire.com/ens/jan2007/ 2007-01-22-09.asp Title: "U.S. Joins in Global Science Gateway" Type of material: Article. Mentions deep Web databases and creation of "Science World."	Deep Web	New product development Added value: science
2/6	Source: PRNewswire URL: www.prnewswire.com/cgi-bin/stories.pl?ACCT= 104&STORY=/www/story/02-05-2007/ 0004520110&EDATE= Title: "Inxight Introduces SmartDiscovery Awareness Server for Oracle® Secure Enterprise Search 10g" Type of material: Article. New product searches Deep Web and public Web with one search.	Deep Web	New product announcement Added value: Business world
2/6	Source: DMReview URL: www.dmreview.com/issues/20070201/ 1075100-1.html Title: *"Third Generation CDI-MDM Solutions"* Author: Aaron Zornes Type of material: Article. New product will search deep Web as well as other sources.	Deep Web	New technology product Added value: Technology market
2/6	Source: Entrepreneurs Stories Blogspot URL: http://entrepreneur-stories.blogspot.com/2007/02/ 6-common-market-research-mistakes-of.html Title: "6 Common Market Research Mistakes of Small Business" Author: Accounter Type of material: Blog (no longer traceable) "Search engines mine only a portion of the web and often the good info you need will be part of the deep web or on a paid search like Lexis Nexis. To save money, visit your local library, business center, or college to gain access to the quality information you need at zero cost."	Deep Web	Article Added value: business research

Continued

▶TABLE 4-1 *Continued*			
Date	Reference	Found Under	Category
2/21	Source: Speaking of Science: Oberlin College Science Library News URL: http://oberlinsciencelibrary.blogspot.com/2007/02/sciencegov-version-40-launched.html Title: "Science.gov Version 4.0 Launched" Type of material: Blog: Speaking of Science—Oberlin College Taken from a Science.gov press release.	Deep Web	New product announcement Added value: Science New search product
2/21	Source: Search Engine Watch.com URL: http://blog.searchenginewatch.com/blog/070214-111207 Title: "Where the Influencers Roam" Author: debbyr Type of material: Blog posting Libraries: Libraries still influence end users. Increasingly, you can remotely search your library's electronic databases and holdings. This previously hidden web of content indices and abstracts is getting exposed by suppliers. Examples include Gale's and ProQuest newspaper archives from the mid-1800s.	Hidden Web	Article Added value: Information people
2/21	Source: HuginGroup. URL: http://www.companynewsgroup.com/communique.asp?co_id=115858 Title: "Digimind Finder Nominated for the European ICT Grand Prize" Type of material: Press release (no longer traceable) "Current Search Solutions Do Not Exploit the Wealth of the Invisible Web."	Invisible Web	New Product Added value: Business

Note: Represents only a sampling of the material received. As noted, some links are no longer accessible.

January through February 2007. The alerts were received and reviewed on a weekly basis and the results were evaluated for inclusion. In some cases, many announcements appear for the same new product and some decision was made about the need to keep duplicating these for this activity. Some articles provide an announcement and introduce new concepts and vocabulary, and all of these elements can be noted.

Table 4-1 gives reference information, date of posting, term that was used to set the alert, and, most important, some categorization of the type of information that was found in the article or blog posting. The Google alerting service does distinguish blog postings from other materials, and a decision can be made to include them or not in this activity. The example table does include them but identifies them as blog postings. The term "Added Value" gives additional ideas that may be gained from reading the material. (For a class activity, a month of alerts should be enough material to start charting for discussions. If the class has the time to keep the chart over several months, this will provide more opportunities to follow discussion themes.)

The following information can be learned from the table. Over this period, eight new product or product information announcements were made demonstrating the importance placed on finding Invisible Web resources. Some of the products mentioned include Science.gov, ChaCha, Digimind Finder, and others. Two guides and three articles came from sources such as Forbes and SearchEngineWatch.com.

Conclusion

Interestingly, many of the resources identified by the Google alerting system fall into the Web-only world and may not have counterparts in the traditional print world found in subscription databases. Also, some of the results tap into blogs, and the value of blogs as information resources is still being sorted out by the academic world. Nevertheless, these entries do show that people who find the Invisible Web may wish to share the information.

ACTIVITY 2: TO ACCESS

Objective

The objective of this activity is to become better able to identify the Invisible Web. A natural question to ask is: How do I know when I am using the Invisible Web? This is a difficult question to answer because the boundaries shift quickly. Looking for the Invisible Web is always a rather fluid pastime. Search tools are always making inroads, and general-purpose search engines index more and more materials. At the same time, Invisible Web content is being created at a greater rate than surface content and changes occur, such as the introduction of new formats not accessible to the search engines.

What can be established is that people are using the Invisible Web when they use many databases, need to fill out a form to receive information, or explore deep and rich Web sites and new formats. The fate of new formats is that if they become popular, search engines will probably try to capture them too, although there will probably be a time delay.

Setup

The bulk of the Invisible Web is composed of database and rich Web site content. This section presents two activities to help identify these two major contributors to the Invisible Web. Some basic premises need to be in place before beginning.

▶ Each general-purpose search engine creates its own version of the Invisible Web according to the decisions it makes about what it will include in its indexing. Search engine coverage varies to an extent that might surprise many, and each search engine's surface Web and Invisible Web are different. (For a comparison of popular search engine coverage, see a study done by Dogpile.Com in 2007, www.dogpile.com.)

▶ If a Web site is not findable through a particular search engine, then it is part of that search engine's Invisible Web. In fact, users should be able to expect that the search engine can help them know what is included and what is not. For this purpose, use Yahoo!'s Site Explorer that promises to identify whether a URL is in their indexing and gives any linking for the site (http://siteexplorer.search.yahoo.com). Google does not have a similar service, but it does offer link checking among its advanced searching options. Link checking might be useful as well since the Google search engine gives a lot of attention to linking. These tools are not conclusive but might help give some indication of what is (surface Web) and what is not (Invisible Web) in the content of the specific search engine. And, of course, using surface Web tools to help identify Invisible Web content illustrates again the close relationship of the two parts of the Web information world.

▶ Each Web page has a Universal Resource Locator (URL) that is unique and should help identify whether it belongs to the surface or Deep Web. Databases that contribute to the size of the Invisible Web provide information dynamically. As part of this process, they present files with temporary URLs. Temporary URLs cannot be used to locate the same material again. The only way to refind the material is to requery that database. The same items found previously will still be there, but with different temporary URLs. Temporary URLs use ?, &, cgi (Common Gateway Interface), and other elements in their construction. The premise is that people should not have to be "techno-mages" to figure it all out. "The easiest way to determine if a Web page is part of the Invisible Web is to examine its URL" (Sherman and Price, 2001:79). A temporary URL cannot be used to find the same item again, and this is a major test of whether a file is invisible or not.

Activity 2, Part 1: How to Identify Temporary URLs

This activity involves collecting database content URLs and identifying them as temporary or fixed to see if they fall into either the surface Web or the Invisible Web.

Up to 90 percent of the Invisible Web is located in databases (Bergman, 2001). The databases that present a problem for general-purpose search engine spiders are those designed to present dynamic content results. This means that the results to answer a query are assembled at the time of the query. When no longer needed, the results disassemble and can be brought together again only as a result of another query similar to the original. Static content databases do not present live searches but rather preassembled answers that have a constant URL to identify them. Dynamic content creates a temporary file with a temporary URL. General-purpose search engines can collect only constant URLs; therefore, database content can be a problem.

Dynamic database construction has its benefits. Such a database saves storage space by not needing to keep and store static or preset search results. Static search records need to be repeated for all searches in which they might apply. A dynamic arrangement requires only one record that can be called up when and for as many times as it is needed. The tradeoff is that searchers must rely on the database's own search function and not a general-purpose search engine search screen. Split-level searching comes into play here. A general-purpose search engine can help locate a database; it just cannot extract information from it. Researchers can navigate the database on their own once it has been identified for them. The first step to testing URLs is to collect them from database content.

Example

Science.gov (www.science.gov) is a specialized search engine that provides access to science-related content provided by U.S. government agencies. The site is hosted by the Department of Energy's Office of Scientific and Technical Information.

This Web site was searched for the term "solar energy." Using the "refine results" feature, the search results were narrowed to 2008 content. The results list screen had the following URL:

> http://www.science.gov/scigov/resultList.html?ssid=4e2aa4d6%3A11e1761ea40%3A-
> 7e75&debugMode=false&searchUrl=search.html%3Fget%3Dtrue%26fullRecord%
> 3Dsolar%2Benergy%26c%3D59%26c%3D57%26c%3D19%26c%3D55%26c%3D17%
> 26c%3D35%26c%3D33%26c%3D34%26c%3D16%26c%3D11%26c%3D38%26c%
> 3D12%26c%3D21%26c%3D41%26c%3D62%26c%3D61%26c%3D22%26c%3D23%
> 26c%3D24%26c%3D25%26c%3D26%26c%3D27%26c%3D29%26c%3D3%26c%
> 3D10%26c%3D1%26c%3D7%26c%3D30%26c%3D6%26c%3D5%26c%3D32%26c%
> 3D31%26c%3D4%26c%3D51%26c%3D52%26c%3D8%26c%3D54&number
> Marked=0&resultPane=0

This is an example of a temporary URL. It cannot be used to locate the search results again. If the same search is performed again, another temporary URL will be given to the search. If we were to test this URL in another browser, the result would be an error message, for example, "We're sorry, there was an error processing your request." This error message may not appear if the smart work-station holds on to the link in case it is needed again during the same session. It may be tried again after shutting down or if another browser is opened to test it.

A general Google search under title and author did not find the exact item and yielded very little in total about the artist. The subscription database WorldCat.org did locate the poster image with the following URL: http://hdl.loc. gov/loc.pnp/cph.3b48842. This link will take the user directly to the image on the Library of Congress site. A Yahoo! Search offered as the first result a link to the WorldCat listing.

Conclusion

Of course, one may question the importance of the information that resides so deeply in the Web site. If it had more value, would it have been easier to find? This is a good question, and perhaps, in this example, it is relevant to challenge the value of the findings. However, with general-purpose search engines overlooking so much information, it can safely be said that the missed information is not all composed of obscure facts, especially as spiders do not evaluate material for indexing.

For examples of deep Web sites, refer to a list of the 60 deepest Web sites, produced by CompletePlanet (CompletePlanet, 2000).

ACTIVITY 3: TO EVALUATE

Objective

The objective of this activity is to compare results from a general-purpose search engine with those from an Invisible Web tool. This activity asks participants to categorize search results by value and type.

Setup

Evaluating search results is an important component of information literacy. Comparing results found using different tools can also be informative, and creating a chart that shows results according to their effectiveness as resources can make an even deeper impression. The comparison of an Invisible Web tool with a general-purpose search engine may highlight both the strengths and weaknesses of each tool and perhaps emphasize the need to know and use more than one tool for research purposes. The process of mapping the results is a way to make users reflect more on their choices.

Example

A search for the subject "solar energy" was made using Google (www.google.com) and INFOMINE (http://infomine.ucr.edu). Google is, of course, a popular search engine. INFOMINE is a scholarly Internet resource often associated with Invisible

Web searching. It provides directory-type annotations as results. Google was searched using its search box; INFOMINE was also searched using a search box but results were modified by using an option to eliminate any fee-based resources. With its directory features, INFOMINE could also have been searched by browsing down through its subject categories.

The first ten results were then organized by categorizing the source by its effectiveness in providing consumer/student-type information for the user. The results were mapped using colors to indicate usefulness or lack thereof.

Sample Charting

The INFOMINE results for "Solar Energy" were categorized as follows:

1. U.S. Department of Energy—Energy Efficiency and Renewable Energy site at www.eere.energy.gov. A section on "Solar Energy Technologies" gave a lot of useful information.
2. Library of Congress Solar Energy Tracer site at www.loc.gov/rr/scitech/tracer-bullets/solartb.html. This site offered bibliographic information only. Not helpful for immediate content.
3. Department of Energy's "A Consumer's Guide to Energy Efficiency and Renewable Energy" at www.eere.energy.gov/consumer/. Part of the first result Web site. Ideal for general information on the topic.
4. Information Bridge—A Department of Energy Search Tool at www.osti.gov/bridge/. A search would need to be made utilizing the site's own search function. Results were a collection of government publications, some very specialized. Limited usefulness.
5. Solar Cooking Archive, a site sponsored by Solar Cookers International, at www.solarcooking.org/. Specialized site, limited usefulness.
6. California Energy Commission site offering information on state energy efficiency standards at www.energy.ca.gov/title24/. Not useful for consumer information.
7. Energy Efficiency and Renewable Energy Database. Because this database is no longer current, the user was taken to the Wayback Machine Web site, which archives materials from sites no longer available. Not helpful because of search steps needed to access information.
8. Solar Radiation Resource Information sponsored by the Renewable Resource Data Center at www.nrel.gov/rredc/. All kinds of resources are organized and linked to from this site. Helpful but will require further searching.
9. Clean Energy Basics—Links through to a National Renewable Energy Laboratory site sponsored by the Department of Energy at www.nrel.gov/learning/. Offers a section on Solar Power Basic that is helpful.

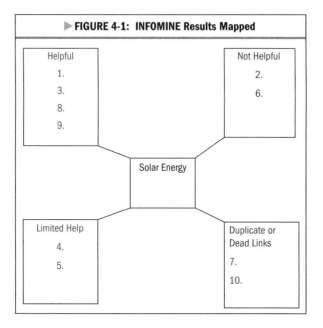

▶ FIGURE 4-1: INFOMINE Results Mapped

10. National Renewable Energy Laboratory (U.S. Department of Energy spon-sored site) at www.nrel.gov/. This is ultimately the same site as the previous link, although the user must browse the site for the information on solar energy.

When these results are mapped, they might appear as shown in Figure 4-1. Google search results were as follows:

1. Wikipedia definition for solar power at http://en.wikipedia.org/wiki/Solar_power. Helpful.
2. SolarEnergy.com at www.solarenergy.com/. A commercial site showing prod-ucts for purchase. Not helpful.
3. Solar Energy International at www.solarenergy.org/. This organizational site offered little information for the consumer. Limited helpfulness.
4. Google News Results for Solar Energy at news.google.com/news?q=solar+energy&hl=en&um=1&ie=UTF-8&sa=X&oi=news_result&resnum=4&ct=title. A link to Google's News Search with current articles on all aspects of the sub-ject. Helpful. Continually updated. Needs to be browsed.
5. ScienceDaily.com—Solar Energy News at www.sciencedaily.com/news/matter_energy/solar_energy. Site offers all kinds of news stories on the sub-ject, continually updated. Helpful but needs to be browsed.
6. Energy Kid's Page at www.eia.doe.gov/kids/energyfacts/sources/renewable/solar.html. Good general information site aimed for children.

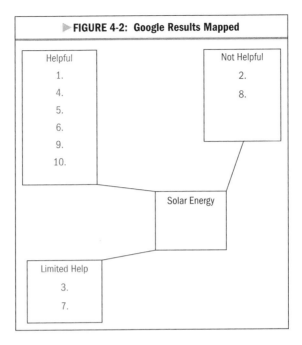

FIGURE 4-2: Google Results Mapped

7. American Solar Energy Society at www.ases.org/. Limited information for consumer/student. Mostly a source of organization news.

8. Solar Energy at www.history.rochester.edu/class/solar/solar.htm. This site is tied in with a class given at the University of Rochester. The site provides links to material that is either specialized or no longer accessible. Not helpful.

9. Energy Story—Chapter 15: Solar Energy at www.energyquest.ca.gov/story/chapter15.html. Good information with links to a whole resource created by California's State Government. Good for children.

10. U.S. Department of Energy—Energy Efficiency and Renewable Energy at www1.eere.energy.gov/solar/. Government-sponsored site, good information under solar categories.

When the results are mapped, they may appear as shown in Figure 4-2.

Conclusion

In this search, both tools provided mixed results, some good and some not helpful. The mapping process can be the occasion for discussions of how different tools work and the kinds of results that are found. Domains can be reviewed. For instance, the INFOMINE tool found many government-sponsored sites while the Google search identified only one. Google provided some split-level searching results by directing people to news reporting services such as their own News Search and the ScienceDaily.com site. These sites must be searched using their own search function. The INFOMINE results tended to be direct information sites.

CONCLUSIONS

These activities presented only some aspects of learning about the Invisible Web. There are many other ways to promote interest, and the Web can provide help. Tools can help generate crossword puzzles or find-a-word games that can be created around search vocabulary. Using them with students can reinforce concepts and expand ideas about research. Information literacy games can be adapted to promote Invisible Web searching and themes. A little searching can show how others promote information literacy in general and promote the Invisible Web in particular.

The next chapter helps complete the exploration of the Invisible Web by providing search tools that can tap its resources.

REFERENCES

Bergman, Michael K. 2001. "The deep Web: Surfacing hidden value." White paper. BrightPlanet. Available: http://brightplanet.com/images/stories/pdf/deepwebwhitepaper.pdf (accessed October 3, 2008).

CompletePlanet. 2000. "List of deep Web sites." Available: http://aip.completeplanet.com/aip-engines/help/largest_engines.jsp (accessed October 3, 2008).

Dogpile.com. 2007. "Different engines, different results: Web searchers not always finding what they're looking for online: A research study by Dogpile.com in collaboration with researchers from the Queensland University and the Pennsylvania State University." Available: www.infospaceinc.com/onlineprod/Overlap-DifferentEnginesDifferentResults.pdf (accessed December 8, 2008).

Krause, Erik Hans. 1936. "Keep Clean." Poster. [Rochester, NY], Federal Art Project. Available: http://hdl.loc.gov/loc.pnp/cph.3b48842 (accessed October 3, 2008).

Sherman, Chris, and Gary Price. 2001. *The Invisible Web: Uncovering Information Sources Search Engines Can't See*. Medford, NJ: CyberAge Books.

▶5

INTERNET RESEARCH
STRATEGIES: AN EXAMPLE

INTRODUCTION

The development of the World Wide Web, easily accessible through general-purpose search engines, and the dominance of Google as the search engine of choice has led students to the widespread illusion that all of their information needs could be resolved on the Web. Several studies show that students feel quite confident in the results of their Web searches and label themselves as information literate (see Chapter 2).

As mentioned in previous chapters, the authors believe that students should be steered toward locating a smorgasbord of sources, a great many of which are part of the "Invisible Web." Instead, today's students prefer to rely on the first ten results of a Google search (see user studies in Chapter 2). Students can learn to dig deeper into the online environment to locate relevant Web resources; this translates into repeated searches on the part of students in various online directories or databases, each with its own interface.

In addition to locating relevant information, the information literate student must also—by the standards established by the American Library Association—be able to evaluate the information located (American Library Association, 1989). Again, the inclusion of the Invisible Web in a search will allow the student to compare the results of a search performed in a general-purpose search engine with the results retrieved from other sources.

USING INVISIBLE WEB CONTENT IN RESEARCH: CASE STUDY

The relevance of using Invisible Web content in research can be illustrated through a fictionalized case study in which sources are retrieved from Google as well as from databases that are part of the Invisible Web. A hypothetical student named Amanda is taking a class in international studies in her second year of college and must write a research paper taking an in-depth look at international development and the recent concept of microfinance.

One approach is for Amanda to initially research the field of microfinance as a whole. Microfinance is a growing object of study within the field of economic development. Microcredit, which is offered by microfinance institutions (MFIs), is defined in the following manner in the 2006 online version of *Encyclopaedia Britannica:*

> Microcredit—a means of extending credit, usually in the form of small loans with no collateral, to nontraditional borrowers such as the poor in rural or undeveloped areas.

Interestingly enough, *Encyclopaedia Britannica*, the well-known, authoritative source, does not contain a definition for "microfinance," whereas *Wikipedia*, "the free encyclopedia that anyone can edit," defines "microcredit" as one part of "microfinance" and gives a more precise definition of the concept of microfinance, at the time this search was performed in November 2006:

> Microfinance is a term used to refer to the activity of provision of financial services to clients who are excluded from the traditional financial system on account of their lower economic status. These financial services will most commonly take the form of loans (see *microcredit*) and savings, though some microfinance institutions will offer other services such as insurance and payment services.

Having completed research about the field as a whole, Amanda will then formulate a specific research question dealing with one aspect of microfinance (e.g., gender and microfinance, poverty and microfinance, etc.) and write a research paper on the final assignment for the course. Actual research for this assignment would probably include print materials, interviews, and other resources. However, since the purpose of this book is to demonstrate the importance of the Invisible Web in information literacy and teaching, the discussion is restricted to online sources.

Amanda, who acts like the majority of her fellow students, will first search Google, the general-purpose search engine of choice (as has been shown in Chapter 2), with the search term "microfinance." Results of her search appear in the following sections along with the results of the same search on "microfinance" repeated in an Invisible Web source, a library subscription database (EBSCOhost), as well as in an online subject directory (INFOMINE). Since, like most students, Amanda does not dig deeper than the first page of results, all of the sample searches are restricted to the first ten results. Other online tools, of course, could have been used, in particular, Google Scholar, which provides access to a body of scholarly literature. However, for the purposes of this fictionalized case study, the searches will be restricted to Google, Academic Search Premier of EBSCOhost, and INFOMINE.

One way to properly evaluate the results found through the various sources that Amanda will search for this paper is to compare these results according to the various criteria used in a checklist for evaluating Web sources, in this case the one developed by Diana Hacker (2002) in her book titled *Research and Documentation in the Electronic Age:*

1. Authorship
2. Sponsorship
3. Purpose and audience
4. Currency

Search Engine Results

A simple search on "microfinance" in Google brings up more than two million results, the first ten of which are illustrated in the screen shot in Figure 5-1 (search performed in January 2006).

The ten results of the Google search on "microfinance" can be categorized as in Table 5-1. The left column of the table describes the Web sites found and the right

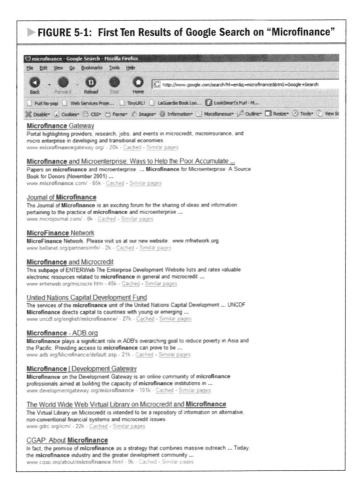

▶ **FIGURE 5-1: First Ten Results of Google Search on "Microfinance"**

▶TABLE 5-1: Description of Web Sites and Checklist Criteria Applied	
Description of Web Sites	Checklist Criteria Applied
FEE-BASED or MEMBERSHIP-BASED (2 items):	
Journal of Microfinance www.microjournal.com	This site is available for subscribers only. (**Purpose** and **Audience** of site)
MicroFinance Network www.mfnetwork.org A global association of the major international MFIs	This site is for members only and requires logon. The members are primarily MFIs. (**Purpose** and **Audience** of site)
MICROFINANCE INDUSTRY-RELATED (3 items):	
Microfinance—ADB.org www.adb.org/Microfinance/default.asp ADB = Asian Development Bank; in business since 1966, a financial institution owned by its 64 members	Although the domain is .org, this site is primarily intended for MFIs. Performs more like a commercial site. (**Sponsorship** and **Audience** of site)
CGAP: About Microfinance www.cgap.org/about/microfinance.html CGAP = Consultative Group to Assist the Poor; a consortium of 33 public and private development agencies	Another .org site that blurs the meaning between a nonprofit and a commercial site, this Web site is for MFIs. (**Sponsorship** and **Audience**) **Currency:** Last updated 2003
Microfinance: Development Gateway www.topics.developmentgateway.org/microfinance A not-for-profit organization started in 2001 by a former head of the World Bank, with the mission of developing Web portal technology for development agencies; offers online training in microfinance through PlaNet University	Who sponsors this site? A former head of the World Bank, one of the biggest players in the microfinance industry. The audience for this Web site is people interested in Web portal technology geared to developmental finance. (**Sponsorship** and **Audience**)
GATEWAYS TO THE INDUSTRY (3 items):	
Microfinance Gateway www.microfinancegateway.org/ In existence since 2000 and managed by CGAP, the same group that maintains the microfinance industry-related Web site noted previously; labels itself as the "most comprehensive source of information for and about the micro industry"	This site is designed to serve the industry. (**Sponsorship** and **Audience**)
The World Wide Web Virtual Library on Microcredit and Microfinance www.gdrc.org/icm Claims to be a repository of information on microcredit and microfinance; belongs to the Global Development Research Center (GDRC), which began in 1995 as a homepage for the Informal Credit Market (ICM), then morphed into the NGO Café and became the GDRC in 2001; offers many links to articles, organizations, banks, and credit institutions. Selections lack objectivity; but, under "New Publications on Microfinance," is a list of newer titles, several of which offer anthropological perspectives on the concept of microfinance, questioning the mainstream view that microfinance does help the poorest of the poor, with links to book reviews that offer citations to works that examine microfinance critically	The Global Development Research Center caters to MFIs. (**Sponsorship** and **Audience**)

Continued

▶ TABLE 5-1 *Continued*	
Description of Web Sites	Checklist Criteria Applied
United Nations Capital Development Fund www.uncdf.org/english/microfinance Focuses on the programs of this UN agency relating to microfinance in terms of funding, technical guidance, and knowledge of "sound microfinance principles and practices"; contains no material critical of microfinance	This is a UN site with links to UN programs only. (**Sponsorship, Purpose,** and **Audience**)
PERSONAL SITES WITH EXCELLENT INFORMATION (2 items):	
Microfinance and Microcredit Enterprise Development Web site www.enterweb.org/microcre.htm Since 1996, maintained by Jean-Claude Lorin, a member of the Canadian International Aid Development Agency; intended as an information clearinghouse on enterprise development; contains some excellent links on microfinance with annotations	Who is Jean-Claude Lorin? What are his credentials for maintaining a Web site on microfinance and microcredit? (**Authorship**)
Microfinance and Microenterprise: Ways to Help the Poor Accumulate Resources www.microfinance.com Collection of academic papers by Mark Schreiner, Senior Scholar at the Center for Social Development at Washington University, St. Louis; includes Schreiner's PhD dissertation, which analyzed the Grameen Bank of Bangladesh, a premier MFI, and the BancoSol of Bolivia, and other papers offering a critical approach to the concept of microfinance	Who is Mark Schreiner? What makes him a knowledgeable source on microfinance? What are his credentials? (**Authorship**)

column gives an evaluation of each Web site according to Hacker's evaluation checklist.

It must be noted at this point how Google ranks its results. Google's claim to fame is PageRank, its page-ranking algorithm whereby a Web site is ranked by the number and quality of the pages that have linked to that particular site. In the past, most search engines rated Web sites by the number of times a search term appeared on its pages. Google founders Larry Page and Sergey Brin felt that a page that was most *linked to*, i.e., most popular, was therefore most worthy of first rank in a results list. This ranking must be kept in mind when analyzing the results from a Google search. Not every student doing research for an academic paper is necessarily looking for the most popular sites on a particular topic. Furthermore, savvy Web designers know how to ensure that their Web page will be ranked high.

A more thorough analysis of the ten results from Google reveals a uniformity in the type of Web sites retrieved. At first glance, the two sites categorized in Table 5-1 as "Personal Sites" seemed the least interesting for research, but evaluation of the content shows that these two Web sites are the only two of the first ten retrieved through Google that bring a more objective and critical viewpoint to the topic of microfinance. The Mark Schreiner site offers access to a majority of his papers as well as a few papers by other authors and contains documents that take an objective look at the field of microfinance and microcredit, something that cannot be said of any of the other eight items on the first page of Google results. The World Wide Web Virtual Library on Microcredit and Microfinance does offer links to a wide array of online resources, primarily to resources useful to microfinance institutions. All of the other sites are truly arms of the microfinance industry and, as such, do not offer an objective viewpoint on the subject. The *Journal of Microfinance*, which might have some critical material on microfinance, is available only by subscription.

A student doing research on this topic should be familiar with these Web sites but cannot rely on them exclusively for a balanced view on the topic of microfinance and microcredit. Thus, analysis of just one page of Google results can be used to explain to students the pitfalls of relying solely on general-purpose search engines. Using a simple checklist for the evaluation of Web sites allows a thorough dissection of the Google results on microfinance.

Library Database Results

Amanda should next continue researching her topic using Invisible Web content. One of the most obvious sources of Invisible Web content is library subscription databases. All libraries today, public or academic, offer access to online subscription databases, which by definition represent collections of information, purposefully selected, electronically stored, and organized for retrieval. A general-purpose search engine cannot retrieve articles from such databases, first, because the information is usually password-protected and, second, because the researcher has to fill out an interactive form to request specific information from the database. A computerized crawler or spider, which indexes Web pages for a general-purpose search engine, can find the homepage of a database but cannot retrieve documents inside it. However, as described in Chapter 7, Google is working in that direction.

One of the most commonly held subscription databases is EBSCOhost, which actually provides access to an array of databases from very general to specialized, subject-specific ones. For the purpose of this research, Amanda chooses Academic Search Premier, as it is one of the most general of EBSCO's periodical databases. She uses the same keyword—"microfinance"—as she used in her earlier Google search. She limits her search to full-text resources to maximize the efficiency, if not necessarily the comprehensiveness, of her search.

The search brings up 124 results, the first ten of which appear in Figure 5-2. Of the ten articles, seven are not useful at all, as they are articles about either personalities or universities donating funds to spearhead microfinance initiatives. However, a feature article in *The Economist*, titled "The Hidden Wealth of the Poor," is represented by the ninth and tenth results in this list. For the most part, these two articles present nonpartisan information about microfinance and are current as of

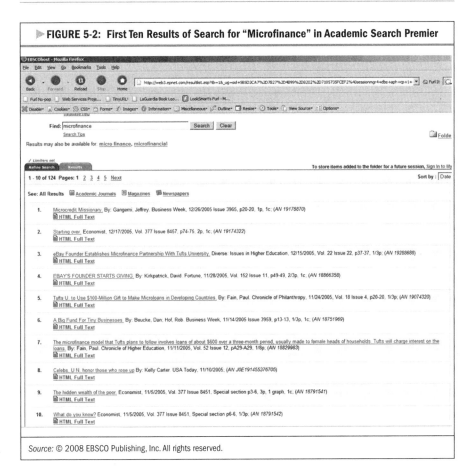

▶ **FIGURE 5-2: First Ten Results of Search for "Microfinance" in Academic Search Premier**

January 2006, when this search was performed. Thus, this search in a subscription database, invisible to general-purpose search engines, has netted one issue of a magazine containing several articles dealing objectively with the topic of microfinance.

Subject Directory Results

If Amanda did not have access to a library subscription database, or simply wanted more information, she could perform a similar search on "microfinance" in an online subject directory such as INFOMINE. Subject directories are "organised lists of Web pages, divided into hierarchically grouped subject areas as a result of human effort" (University of Tasmania, 2006). They are available to anyone who has access to an Internet connection. Specifically, "INFOMINE is a virtual library of Internet resources relevant to faculty, students, and research staff at the university level" (INFOMINE homepage, 2006). It has always been associated with the Invisible Web as a source for tapping content not available through general-purpose search engines.

The results of Amanda's search for "microfinance" in INFOMINE appear in the appendix at the end of this chapter. The search retrieved a total of 11 Web sites associated with microfinance. These 11 results, some of which overlap with items on the first page of the Google results described above, can be analyzed as shown in Table 5-2.

Analysis of her searches for "microfinance" using Google, Academic Search Premier, and INFOMINE make it obvious to Amanda that she cannot afford to limit herself to a single search in a single interface. To round out her research paper and ensure that she has found enough appropriate information, Amanda must repeat the

▶TABLE 5-2: Analysis of Web Sites and Checklist Criteria Applied	
Analysis of Web Sites	Checklist Criteria Applied
GATEWAYS TO THE INDUSTRY (1 item)	
2. The Virtual Library on Microcredit http://gdrc.org/icm/index.html Also found using Google.	The GDRC caters to MFIs. (**Sponsorship**)
MICROFINANCE-INDUSTRY RELATED (1 item)	
1. Consultative Group to Assist the Poorest (CGAP) www.cgap.org/ Also found using Google.	Although a .org, this site is geared primarily toward MFIs. (**Audience** and **Sponsorship**) **Currency:** Last updated in 2003
DIRECTORIES (4 items)	
10. Biz/ed Internet Catalogue http://catalogue.bized.ac.uk/ A free, online service for students and teachers in the areas of business, economics, and accounting; a search for "microfinance" yields 17 Web sites of major industry players	This site offers good annotations and lists of relevant keywords; includes access to the papers of M. Schreiner, who has written analytical papers on microfinance; and is intended for students and researchers. (**Purpose** and **Audience**)
4. Directory of Development Organizations www.devdir.org/ Web version of the 2006 edition of "Directory of Development Organizations," arranged by geographic areas; labels itself the "resource guide to development organizations and the Internet"	Up-to-date list of organizations (**Currency**) to be used by people in the development field. (**Audience**)
7. International Government Organizations www.library.northwestern.edu/govpub/resource/internat/igo.html A Web guide put together by the Library at Northwestern University, Evanston, Illinois	This site was created for the Northwestern University community. (**Audience** and **Purpose**)
8. Sustainable Development: The World Wide Web Virtual Library www.ulb.ac.be/ceese/meta/sustvl.html "Comprehensive list of Internet sites dealing with sustainable development"; maintained by the Center for Economic Studies on the Environment located at the Université Libre de Bruxelles	Maintained on a university server (**Audience**), the site is hard to use and is mainly a directory of organizations. (**Purpose**)

Continued

▷ TABLE 5-2 *Continued*	
Analysis of Web Sites	Checklist Criteria Applied
PERSONAL SITES WITH EXCELLENT INFORMATION (1 item)	
5. ENTERWeb The Enterprise Development Site 6. ENTERWeb Small Business Portal www.enterweb.org Two entries in INFOMINE that are the same, the Web portal clearinghouse on small businesses, created and maintained by Jean-Claude Lorin, a Canadian who works for the International Aid Development Agency. Entry 5 = link that focuses on microfinance and microcredit; also found using Google	Although this is a personal site, the author has been working in the development field for years and is fully qualified. (**Sponsorship**) The site is aimed at professionals, academics, and students interested in enterprise development. (**Purpose** and **Audience**)
DIGITAL LIBRARY (1 item)	
3. Humanity Development Library www.sadl.uleth.ca/nz/cgi-bin/library?a=p&p=about&c=hdl Part of the Humanity Libraries Project, headquartered in Antwerp, Belgium; provides access to over 1,200 publications in the field of development; an extremely useful tool offering books and other publications that looks critically at the field of microfinance For example, offers full-text access to a book by Susan Johnson and Ben Rogaly, titled *Microfinance and Poverty Reduction*, which analyzes whether microloans really do help the poorest Found only through INFOMINE	This site offers books, reports, and magazine content containing information on the alleviation of world poverty. (**Purpose**) It is hard to navigate but provides access to excellent information on microfinance.
NOT VERY USEFUL (2 items)	
9. Egypt: U.S. Agency for International Development www.usaid-eg.org A USAID site for a particular region; included in the search results because of section on economic assistance to Egypt	This site looks at a single geographical area for USAID and is not useful for a paper on microfinance. (**Sponsorship**)
11. Economic Reconstruction and Development in South East Europe http://seerecon.org Another site on a particular geographic region, this one from the European Union	This site concentrates on one geographic area for one organization and is not useful for research on microfinance. (**Sponsorship**)

search in various interfaces, using a variety of Invisible Web content. Faculty members could require this level of research on a much smaller scale in any discipline.

Narrowing the Search

However, Amanda has still not formulated a question regarding a specific aspect of microfinance as requested by her professor. In doing the general research on the topic of microfinance, she has seen constant referral to one aspect of microfinance, namely the alleviation of poverty through microcredit, the extension of small loans to people, usually women, too poor to qualify for traditional bank loans. Amanda decides to redefine her topic, narrowing it to a question: How does microfinance alleviate poverty? She now needs to do new searches, using a combination of two keyword terms: "microfinance" and "poverty." Since the sources Amanda originally found on Google, using the basic Google search for "microfinance," were primarily directories or gateways rather than actual papers discussing the problem of microfinance, Amanda hopes that, by redoing her search in Google with the two keywords "microfinance" and "poverty," she will find more focused resources. The results of her search appear in Figure 5-3.

The first link is an entry in a blog dated March 2005. Although the entry is brief, and not meaty enough for Amanda to use in her research paper, the blog offers several interesting links, the first one to a news analysis from United Press International in which the concept of microfinance is compared to a Band-Aid solution to poverty. The second result offers a link to a PDF file of a full-text article

---

▶ **FIGURE 5-3: Results of Google Search for "Microfinance and Poverty"**

A Constrained Vision: **Microfinance and poverty** alleviation
Microfinance and poverty alleviation. **Microfinance**, the practice of giving very small loans to poor people to help them start or expand their businesses, ...
aconstrainedvision.blogspot.com/2005/02/microfinance-and-poverty-alleviation.html - 24k - Cached - Similar pages

[PDF] Analysis of the Effects of **Microfinance** on **Poverty** Reduction
File Format: PDF/Adobe Acrobat - View as HTML
The impact of **microfinance** on **poverty** alleviation has recently gained a ... **Microfinance** reduces **poverty** by increasing per capital consumption among program ...
www.nyu.edu/wagner/public_html/cgi-bin/workingPapers/wp1014.pdf - Similar pages

[PDF] Impact of **Microfinance** on **Poverty** Alleviation: What Does Emerging ...
File Format: PDF/Adobe Acrobat - View as HTML
microfinance as an effective tool for alleviating. **poverty**. Since much of the impetus behind this. large and increasing support for **microfinance** hinges ...
www.ifpri.org/themes/mp05/bnef/mp05_bnef02.pdf - Similar pages

Microfinance and Poverty Reduction in Asia: What is the Evidence?
Paper surveying evidence from studies of MFIs looking at impact and cost-effectiveness issues in **poverty** reduction.
www.adbi.org/research-paper/2003/01/01/37.microfinance.and.poverty.reduction.in.asia/ - 22k - Cached - Similar pages

    Great Expectations: **Microfinance and Poverty** Reduction in Asia and ...
    This paper compares experience with **microfinance** lending in Asia and Latin America and assesses its impact on the very poor.
    www.adb.org/discussion-paper/2004/11/24/817.microfinance.poverty.asia.latin/ - 22k - Cached - Similar pages

EXECUTIVE SUMMARY: Financing **Microfinance** for **Poverty** Reduction
Financing **Microfinance** for **Poverty** Reduction. David S. Gibbons Managing Director. CASHPOR Financial and Technical Services. Jennifer W. Meehan ...
www.microcreditsummit.org/papers/abstract_ch5.html - 3k - Cached - Similar pages

Microfinance and Poverty Reduction
The increased availability of microfinance facilities is no 'magic bullet' for **poverty** reduction. Many other changes are also needed, but **microfinance** can ...
www.ifad.org/media/pack/**microfinance**.htm - 16k - Cached - Similar pages

[PPT] **Microfinance and Poverty**
File Format: Microsoft Powerpoint 97 - View as HTML
Microfinance and Poverty. Monique Cohen. **Microfinance** Opportunities. November 2002 ... Improving **Poverty** Impact of **Microfinance**? Market-Led **Microfinance** ...
www.iadb.org/int/DRP/ing/Red3/documents/CohenMicrofinanzasy11-02eng.pps - Similar pages

Microfinance Development Strategy - ADB.org
Microfinance can be a critical element of an effective poverty reduction strategy. ... **Microfinance and Poverty** Reduction. Oxfam, Oxford. ...
www.adb.org/Documents/Policies/Microfinance/**microfinance**0100.asp - 30k - Cached - Similar pages

Analysis of the effects of **microfinance** on **poverty** reduction: overview
Are **microfinance** programmes effective in reaching the poorest? There is evidence to support the positive impact of **microfinance** on **poverty** reduction, ...
www.eldis.org/static/DOC10964.htm - 27k - Cached - Similar pages

Try your search again on Google Book Search

written by J. Morduch of New York University on the effects of microfinance on poverty reduction. This same article is also available through another interface in the tenth result. Amanda can definitely use this source in her paper. The third link is a position paper sponsored by the International Food Policy Research Institute, whereas the seventh is from International Food for Agricultural Development, both preaching to the MFIs. The fourth and fifth links are both from the Asian Development Bank Institute, here offering access to two full-text documents that are critical of the whole concept of microfinance and thus rounding out Amanda's research. The eighth and tenth links are not useful at all and the ninth link is dead at this time.

To further explore her topic in a magazine and journal subscription database, Amanda would repeat her search for the two keywords, "microfinance" and "poverty," in Academic Search Premier, now connecting them with the Boolean operator "and" and, in this case, not limiting her results to full-text material. Amanda's search statement, "microfinance and poverty," retrieves 48 items, the first eight of which are presented in Figure 5-4.

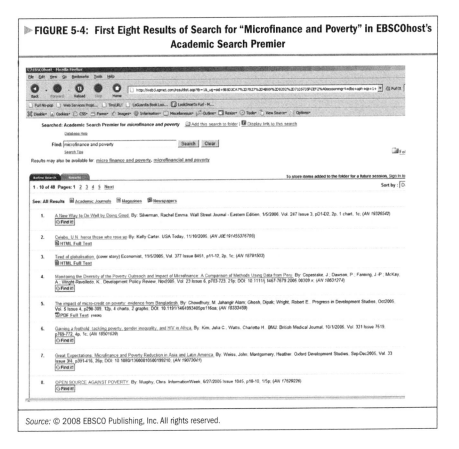

▶ **FIGURE 5-4: First Eight Results of Search for "Microfinance and Poverty" in EBSCOhost's Academic Search Premier**

Seven of the eight articles in these Academic Search Premier results can be used in a paper on how microfinance reduces poverty. The second entry is the only result that is not appropriate. The seventh entry is an article called "Great Expectations: Microfinance and Poverty Reduction in Asia and Latin America" and published in a journal titled *Oxford Development Studies.* In it, the author, John Weiss, argues that the concepts of microfinance and microcredit do not necessarily alleviate poverty. The article has a useful bibliography that can lead Amanda to further studies regarding the worthiness of microfinance and microcredit. At this juncture of the research process, Amanda will have to use her critical thinking skills to decide which sources to incorporate into her research paper. She needs to analyze each entry carefully to make sure she understands the viewpoint of each of the nine articles: who sponsors the writer, whose point of view is given (that of the MFIs or that of their critics), etc. These are some of the questions Amanda must ask herself by following the checklist criteria used previously, namely sponsorship, authorship, purpose, and audience.

CONCLUSIONS

This analysis of searches repeated in a general-purpose search engine and various Invisible Web content interfaces is, of course, lengthy. Discipline faculty can probably not allocate the time for such detailed analysis of the research undertaken by students in the class. However, a shorter activity along the same principles is feasible. Students can be asked to demonstrate how they obtained certain sources for their research papers. They can evaluate the results of their searches in terms of the criteria laid out earlier in this chapter (authorship, sponsorship, purpose and audience, currency) or those of other checklists and standards, which abound on the Web. This exercise is one way to prevent all results from coming through a single search interface (usually a general-purpose search engine). The results of the analysis can be generated in the form of a table or a graph that is easy to read at a glance. Figure 5-5 examines the search Amanda did on "microfinance" in Google, Academic Search Premier, and INFOMINE.

Discipline faculty can request such an analysis, or a partial one, before giving the final okay for the research paper. This extra step would allow the faculty to redirect students to more appropriate sources if needed. This process would bring a touch of information literacy into every classroom.

How does this analysis of using Invisible Web content in a research paper fulfill the information literacy standards formulated by the American Library Association? The fictionalized case study on microfinance discussed in detail in this chapter provides concrete evidence that students should not submit research papers in which all the sources have been gleaned using a general-purpose search engine. Students must be become familiar with the literature of their field, their discipline, their topic

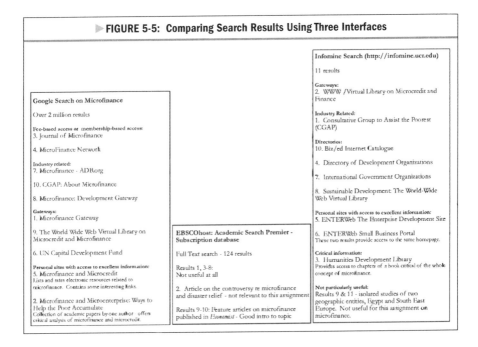

▶ FIGURE 5-5: Comparing Search Results Using Three Interfaces

and can do so only by becoming familiar with the notion of the Invisible Web. Using the Invisible Web may mean nothing more than using a subscription database from the home library's Web page. It can also translate into a search in a specialized subject directory, a look at a pathfinder created about the field, etc. The student must be able to show how the needed information was located and evaluated.

REFERENCES

About INFOMINE. 2006. INFOMINE homepage. Available: http://infomine.ucr.edu/about/about.shtml (accessed October 9, 2008).

American Library Association. 1989. *Presidential Committee on Information Literacy: Final Report.* Available: www.ala.org/ala/mgrps/divs/acrl/publications/whitepapers/presidential.cfm (accessed December 7, 2008).

Encyclopaedia Britannica Online. 2006. Academic ed., s.v. "Microcredit." Available: http://search.eb.com (accessed October 27, 2006).

Hacker, Diane. 2002. *Research and Documentation in the Electronic Age,* 3rd ed. Boston: Bedford/St. Martin's.

University of Tasmania Library. 2006. *Library eTutor Glossary,* s.v. "Subject Directory." Available: www.utas.edu.au/library/etutor/glossary.html (accessed October 9, 2008).

Wikipedia: The Free Encyclopedia. 2006. s.v. "Microfinance." Available: http://en.wikipedia.org/wiki/Microfinance (accessed October 27, 2006).

APPENDIX: SEARCH ON "MICROFINANCE" IN INFOMIME

Search Results   Page 1 of 5

Scholarly Internet Resource Collections

Search Results   All Subject Categorie

Query: **microfinance**
Expert-selected Resources Found: **11**   **Modify Search**   **New Search**
Add Robot-selected Resources? ⬚ OK
                                                                      Titles Display

Result Pages: 1

1. Consultative Group to Assist the Poorest (CGAP)

                                                                                Score: ⸲

The Consultative Group to Assist the Poorest (CGAP) is a consortium of 29 bilateral and multilateral donor
agencies who support microfinance. Their mission is to improve the capacity of microfinance institutions to delive
flexible, high-quality financial services to the very poor on a sustainable basis.

CGAP serves the microservice institiutions, donors and the microfinance industry through the development of
technical tools and services, delivery of training, strategic advice and technical assistance, and action research c
innovations. Site includes: The Microfinance Gateway, a database with over 400 websites related to microfinanc

[More Info...]   [Comment on this resourc

2. The Virtual Library on Microcredit

                                                                                Score: ⸲

This site provides strategies, tools, case studies, bibliographies, links to related web sites, and other valuable
resources pertaining to microcredit. "Topically, the following are covered: informal credit, microcredit, community
based finance, community organization, participation, roles of NGOs, credit access for women, microenterprises,
linking savings and credit, Capacity Building for Microfinance, credit unions and cooperatives etc. The range of
topics are kept flexible and relevant to the overall theme of microcredit. 'Microcredit' includes both credit and
savings. Urban and rural areas of low-income and transitional economies in Asia, Africa, Latin America and
Central/Eastern Europe are the primary focus."

[More Info..]   [Comment on this resourc

3. The Humanity Development Library

                                                                                Score

"The Humanity Development Library is a large collection of practical information aimed at helping reduce poverty
increasing human potential, and providing a practical and useful education for all. This version, 2.0, contains 1,2:
publications -- books, reports, and magazines--in various areas of human development, from agricultural practice
to economic policies, from water and sanitation to society and culture, from education to manufacturing, from
disaster mitigation to micro-enterprises. It contains a total of 160,000 pages and 30,000 images, which if printed
would weigh 340 kg and cost US$20,000. It is available here and on CD-ROM at US$6 for distribution in
developing countries.

The objective of the Humanity Libraries Project is to provide all involved in development, well-being and basic
needs with access to a complete library of around 3,000 multidisciplinary books containing practical knowhow an
ideas." Major sections of this digital library include:

http://infomine.ucr.edu/cgi-bin/canned_search   3/28/2006

Search Results   Page 2 of 5

01.00 General reference

02.00 Sustainable Development, International cooperation, Projects; NGO, Organizations, Poverty and Hunger Alleviation, Basic Human Needs

03.00 Economics, Economic policies, Finance, Trade, Structural Adjustment

04.00 Business, Micro-entreprises, Management, Marketing, Finance, Microfinance, Cooperatives

05.00 Politics, Public administration, Law and Legislation, Peace, Human Rights

06.00 Society, Culture, Community, Woman, Youth, Population

07.00 Education and Training

08.00 Communication, Information and Documentation

09.00 Transport

10.00 Science, Research and Technology

11.00 Ecology, Biodiversity, Natural resources, Environment, Waste Disposal

12.00 Water, Sanitation and Sewage Disposal

13.00 Health, Nutrition, Medicine

14.00 Agriculture and Food Processing

15.00 Plant and Crop Production, Protection, and Processing

16.00 Animal Husbandry and Animal Product Processing

17.00 Fishery and Aquaculture

18.00 Forestry and Agroforestry

19.00 Industry, Manufacture and Services

20.00 Energy , Renewable energies, Household energy

21.00 Settlements, Housing, Building - Infrastructure Construction (Roads etc)

22.00 Disasters, Disaster Mitigation, Humanitarian and Food Aid, Humanitarian Interventions, Refugees

23.00 Development Periodicals and Magazines

24.00 Resources, Product Lists, Catalogues, Internet Sites

[More Info...]   [Comment on this resourc

4. Directory of Development Organizations

                                                                              Score
"The Directory lists 25,000 contacts of organizations that offer (non-) financial support, market access, informatio

Search Results

and advice to the enterprise and poverty-reducing sectors in low-income countries. Contact details include the organization's mail and street address, telephone and fax numbers, e-mail address and Web page details, if available. This Directory is intended to provide a comprehensive source of reference for development practitione researchers, donor employees, and policymakers who are interested in private sector development and poverty alleviation, particularly in low-income countries."

Categories of organization include:
1. International Organizations : including e.g. UN, World Bank, IaDB, AfDB, AsDB;
2. Government : Ministries, Government Institutions, Planning Agencies, Donor Agencies;
3. Private Sector Support Organizations : Chambers of Commerce and Industry, Fairtrade Organizations, Trade Promotion Organizations;
4. Finance Institutions : Central Banks, National Development Banks, Commercial Banks, Credit Unions, Finance Houses;
5. Training and Research Organizations : Universities, Research Centres and Institutions, Training Institutes;
6. Non-Governmental Organizations (NGOs) / Private Development Organizations (PDOs) : Microfinance Institutions, Development Programmes and Projects, Development Foundations and Associations, Membership Development Organizations, Church Development Organizations;
7. Development Consulting Firms;
8. Information Providers : Newsletters/Journals, Publishers, Web Resources, Databases;
9. Grantmakers : Fundraising, Charity and Philanthropic Organizations.

[More Info...]   [Comment on this resourc

5. ENTERWeb The Enterprise Development Website

                                                                                     Score:

"ENTERWeb is an exceptional resource for professionals, academics and students interested in enterprise development in the global economy. Rated links to web sites on timely topics (technology transfer, finance, business law, education and training) are abundant. Links to business information for developing countries and emerging markets is here, too (Latin America, Asia, Africa and Europe). This award winning site also has discussion groups, conference and seminar information, business news and more."

[More Info...]   [Comment on this resourc

6. ENTERWeb Small Business Portal: entrepreneurship, business, international trade, finance, employment

                                                                                     Score:

"ENTERWeb is an annotated meta-index and information clearinghouse on enterprise development, business, finance, international trade and the economy in this new age of cyberspace and globalization.The main focus is (micro, small and medium scale enterprises, cooperatives, community economic development, both in developed and developing countries. ENTERWeb lists and rates Internet resources in these areas, and complements searc engines by providing shortcuts in identifying important sources of information."

[More Info...]   [Comment on this resourc

7. International Governmental Organizations

                                                                                     Score:

This directory connects to the websites of international governmental organizations. Particular emphasis is given agencies of the United Nations and the European Union.

[More Info...]   [Comment on this resourc

8. Sustainable Development: The World-Wide Web Virtual Library

Score:

This is an extensive virtual library "of internet sites dealing with sustainable development, including organisations projects and activities, electronic journals, libraries, references and documents, databases, directories or metadatabases."

[More Info...]   [Comment on this resourc

9. Egypt : U.S. Agency for International Development

Score:

USAID presents information about U.S. economic assistance to Egypt and the results economic assistance programs. Categories on the web site are:
---Economic growth
---Promoting democracy
---Population and health
---Environmental protection
---U.S.-Egyptian Partnership for Economic Growth and Development
---Development links
Among the Development links is the U.S. Embassy in Egypt with information on investing in Egypt.

[More Info...]   [Comment on this resourc

10. The Biz/ed Internet Catalogue

Score:

The Biz/ed Internet Catalogue aims to provide a reliable source of selected, high quality Internet information for students, researchers and practitioners in the areas of business, management and economics. The Internet Catalogue contains over 3013 resources. Topics covered:

- Accounting Profession
- Business - General
- Economics - General
- Financial Economics
- Higher Education
- Human Resources
- Macroeconomics
- Management - General
- Marketing
- Mathematical Economics
- Organisational Management
- Production and the Firm
- Tourist Industry
- Trade and Commerce

[More Info...]   [Comment on this resourc

11. Economic Reconstruction and Development in South East Europe

Score:

Background information on the European Union's policy toward South East Europe (Bulgaria, Romania, Albania, Bosnia and Herzegovina, Croatia, Macedonia, Serbia and Montenegro), progress of countries toward EU accession, details on international assistance to the region, current news, and regional development reports. Als a reference section contains:
--Press releases
--Speeches and statements

http://infomine.ucr.edu/cgi-bin/canned_search   3/28/2006

►6

A SAMPLER OF TOOLS FOR MINING THE INVISIBLE WEB

INTRODUCTION

This chapter examines in greater detail a sampling of tools for searching the Invisible Web. It is impossible to keep up with all of the tools used to mine the Invisible Web as new resources emerge daily. The list in this section, therefore, does not represent a definitive list of tools but simply highlights examples of the various types of resources available to the researcher. The tools examined are directories, databases, and search engines.

GENERAL SUBJECT DIRECTORIES

The first category of tools used to mine the Deep or Invisible Web are subject directories that offer the ability to research a large topic, and then its subtopics. Directories allow the user to get an overview of the subject matter through a hierarchical arrangement in which the information provided goes from general to specific. Human beings, unlike the robotic crawlers or spiders that power search engines, create directories. Directories are hybrid products that usually retrieve both surface Web and Invisible Web sources, culling the best from both. The following text describes a selection of the better-known subject directories.

Librarians' Internet Index (www.lii.org)

Librarians' Internet Index (LII) (see Figure 6-1) is one of the best-known general directories on the Web. It "is a publicly-funded Web site and weekly newsletter serving California, the nation, and the world" (www.lii.org/cs/lii/print/htdocs/about_overview.htm). The site includes more than 20,000 annotated entries organized into 14 major categories as follows:

1. Arts and Humanities
2. Business

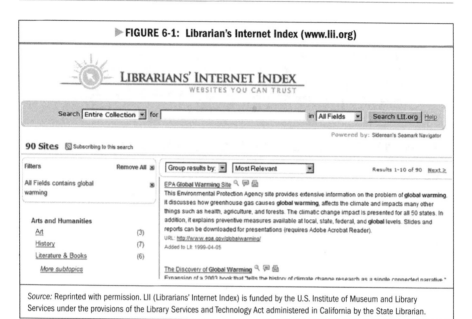

▶ **FIGURE 6-1: Librarian's Internet Index (www.lii.org)**

Source: Reprinted with permission. LII (Librarians' Internet Index) is funded by the U.S. Institute of Museum and Library Services under the provisions of the Library Services and Technology Act administered in California by the State Librarian.

3. Computers
4. Government
5. Health
6. Home and Housing
7. Law
8. Media
9. People
10. Ready Reference and Quick Facts
11. Recreation
12. Regions of the World
13. Science
14. Society and Social Science

Every Web site is evaluated by librarians. Unfortunately in 2006, LII lost 50 percent of its funding and is adjusting its services accordingly.

A search on a broad topic such as "global warming" retrieves 90 annotated sites. The topic is subdivided by a list of filters on the left of the screen with, in parentheses, the number of Web sites that fall within each of these subcategories (see screenshot). These filters can be browsed to narrow a topic. A search can also be limited to "Current Results" rather than the "Entire Collection." In addition, LII, as with most directories today, offers keyword searching functionality to complement directory results. However, LII searches only the description of Web pages, whereas general-purpose search engines crawl through several levels within a Web site. Subject directories such as LII are more manageable than general-purpose

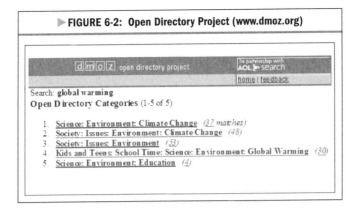

▶FIGURE 6-2: Open Directory Project (www.dmoz.org)

search engines in terms of the number of Web sites a search retrieves as well as in the assured quality of those Web sites. LII, a California product, has a slant toward resources from that state.

The Open Directory Project (www.dmoz.org)

The Open Directory Project (see Figure 6-2) claims to be "the largest, most comprehensive human-edited directory of the Web. It is constructed and maintained by a vast, global community of volunteer editors" (www.dmoz.org/about.html).

A search on "global warming" brings up five major categories, each subdivided further (see screenshot). Every source is briefly annotated. The difference between this directory and the Librarian's Internet Index is that the Open Directory Project is compiled by volunteers who choose the sites and evaluate them, whereas LII is staffed by public librarians.

INFOMINE: Scholarly Internet Resource Collections (http://infomine.ucr.edu)

A third general subject directory available on the Web is INFOMINE, a virtual library of Internet sources for students and faculty. This resource contains nine major categories (see Figure 6-3) as well as a search engine for the sources within the directory. Academic librarians evaluate each source for inclusion. INFOMINE includes more than Web sites: "databases, electronic journals, electronic books, bulletin boards, mailing lists, online library card catalogs, articles, directories of researchers, and many other types of information" (http://infomine.ucr.edu/about/). Not all sources retrieved are free; an icon of a dollar sign warns users if a fee is involved. INFOMINE is the product of several participating colleges led by the Library of the University of California at Riverside. Compared to LII and the Open Directory Project, which are oriented toward the general public, INFOMINE is an academic

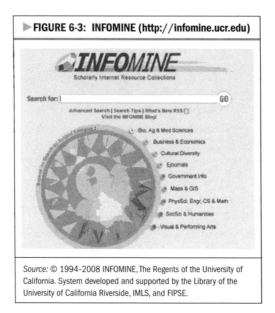

▶ FIGURE 6-3: INFOMINE (http://infomine.ucr.edu)

Source: © 1994–2008 INFOMINE, The Regents of the University of California. System developed and supported by the Library of the University of California Riverside, IMLS, and FIPSE.

source. It offers not only search options but browse options that help students narrow a topic. INFOMINE also offers an advanced search screen that makes it possible to search across all nine disciplines while still limiting searches by field.

Other Subject Directories of Interest

▶ About.com (www.about.com) "is an online neighborhood of hundreds of helpful experts we call 'Guides'" (www.aboutmediakit.com/guides/index.html). Owned by the *New York Times*, this directory is useful for popular topics.

▶ BUBL Information Service: Catalogue of Internet Resources (http://bubl. ac.uk/) is a British site that includes Web resources in all academic subject areas.

▶ Internet Public Library (www.ipl.org/). Started in 1995 at the University of Michigan School of Information, IPL moved to Drexel in 2007. It describes itself as "a public service organization and a learning/teaching environment" (www.ipl.org/div/about/).

▶ Intute (www.intute.ac.uk/) provides access to Web resources in Science, Engineering and Technology, Arts and Humanities, Social Sciences, and Health and Life Sciences, with a British slant. Every source is evaluated by a subject specialist.

▶ The WWW Virtual Library (http://vlib.org/) is considered the oldest catalog on the Web. Available in different languages, it is maintained by volunteers.

▶ Yahoo! Directory (http://dir.yahoo.com/), created in 1994, was one of the earliest subject directories. Although Yahoo! has become a portal with a search engine, one can still use its directory.

DATABASES

Most people have probably used a database, even without knowing it. A database is an online collection of data organized for retrieval. Databases come in various categories—general versus subject databases, free versus subscription. A student affiliated with a public library or a university has access to subscription databases that, by their nature, will always be part of the Invisible Web. Two well-known subscription databases are LexisNexis Academic, an excellent resource for newspaper articles and legal materials, and Academic Search Premier from EBSCOhost, a massive source of magazine and journal articles. However, more and more, it is possible to find databases available on the free Web. Google has recently made some inroads into that area, as explained in Chapter 7. Google Scholar retrieves a mixture of resources: citations, abstracts, and some full-text articles and papers. For students affiliated with an academic institution, a link resolver program can provide full-text access to some of the material cited in Google Scholar but actually made available through the university's full-text subscription databases. Some databases offer citations and abstracts only, whereas others provide full text and many offer a mixture of the two.

THOMAS (http://thomas.loc.gov/)

The Library of Congress THOMAS database (see Figure 6-4) offers "in the spirit of Thomas Jefferson" legislative information to the public at large. One can search through bills and resolutions, treaties, committee reports, and the *Congressional Record*; look for presidential nominations of various government officials; and find links to other government resources.

LexisNexis Academic (www.lexisnexis.com)

LexisNexis Academic, by comparison, is a subscription database available through an affiliation. The search options within the "Legal" tab in LexisNexis are prolific, as shown in Figure 6-5.

The searches, all full-text, will bring up all American case law, state or federal, as well as the federal and state codes, tax law, patent law, Canadian court cases, Canadian legislation, and the laws of European, Commonwealth, and foreign nations. Many full-text newspaper articles from around the world on the topics listed previously are also retrievable through LexisNexis Academic. Keyword searching is available as well as article title, journal title, author, or legal citation searches. Searches can be modified by date or narrowed to a particular source.

Other interesting comparisons can be made between a free medical database such as PubMed (www.ncbi.nlm.nih.gov/pubmed/), available through the U.S.

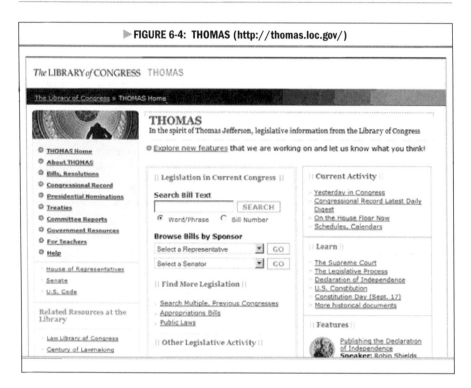

▶ FIGURE 6-4: THOMAS (http://thomas.loc.gov/)

▶ FIGURE 6-5: LexisNexis Academic (www.lexisnexis.com)

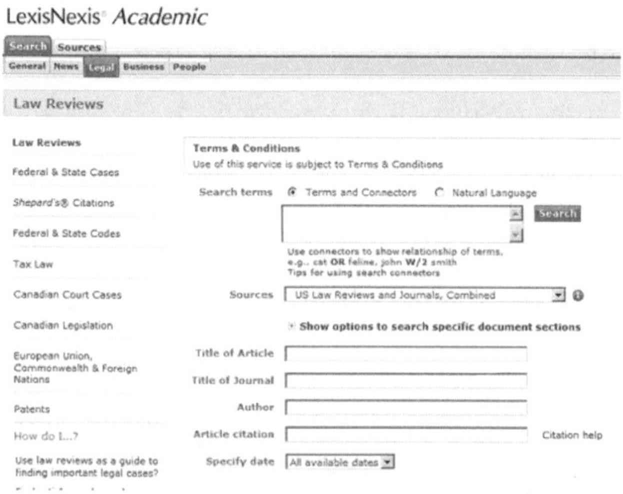

National Library of Medicine and the National Institutes of Health, and the subscription database CINAHL Plus with Full Text (Cumulated Index for Allied Health Literature), available through EBSCOhost. PubMed "includes over 18 million citations from MEDLINE and other life science journals for biomedical articles back to the 1968. PubMed includes links to full-text articles and other related resources" (www.ncbi. nlm.nih.gov/pubmed/). CINAHL is a full-text database for more than 750 journals.

In the field of business, Hoover's (www.hoovers.com/free/), a Dun & Bradstreet company, offers free information on companies, industries, and people. More information can be obtained via subscription. As explained earlier in this chapter, students who have an affiliation can obtain more in-depth, full-text articles on business companies through subscription databases. One example is the Business Company Resource Center, a Gale product that offers not only company profiles but also news and magazine articles about the companies, histories, investment reports, financials, rankings, products, industry overviews, and information about associations.

ERIC—Education Resources Information Center (www.eric.ed.gov/)

In the realm of education, ERIC, Education Resources Information Center (www.eric.ed.gov/), is a bibliographic and full-text database for education research and information (see Figure 6-6). Although the bulk of the sources comprise articles from journals, ERIC also provides access to books, conference papers, and various types of technical reports. The Web site redesigned in summer 2008 now

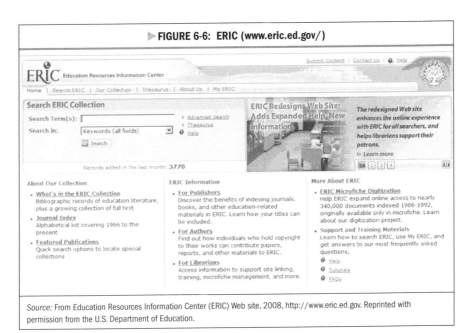

▷**FIGURE 6-6: ERIC (www.eric.ed.gov/)**

Source: From Education Resources Information Center (ERIC) Web site, 2008, http://www.eric.ed.gov. Reprinted with permission from the U.S. Department of Education.

allows faster navigation and provides better help screens. ERIC is an excellent source for teachers, librarians, or anyone doing research in the field of education.

To take research in education a step further, a user can access, through a public or academic affiliation, this same ERIC database through the EBSCOhost interface. A search repeated in EBSCOhost's ERIC database will retrieve the same documents as in www.eric.ed.gov/, with many now available in full text. Full text is made feasible through a local link resolver program that provides full-text access to documents irrespective of the database in which they are found.

OAIster.org (www.oaister.org)

Many organizations now provide access to their own digital repositories of institutional materials in order to make their resources freely available. OAIster is an example of a collaborative effort to provide access to such collections through a common interface (see Figure 6-7).

OAIster describes itself as a "union catalog" of digital resources. It makes use of the Open Archives Initiative Protocol for Metadata Harvesting (OAI-PMH). OAIster was developed in 2001 through collaboration between the University of Michigan and the University of Illinois at Urbana-Champaign to access Invisible

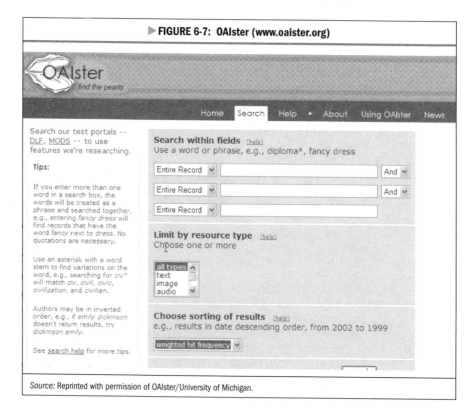

▶ FIGURE 6-7: OAIster (www.oaister.org)

Source: Reprinted with permission of OAIster/University of Michigan.

Web material located in institutional repositories, online journals, and digital libraries. Its content is scholarly and includes international resources.

A search on "global warming" retrieved 3,709 results with sources that include policy papers, conference presentations, articles from digital collections, and foreign language materials. The information for each item in the results list includes not only citation information but also resource type, format, and URL. Results are also broken down on the left side of the screen by contributing organization. The OAIster search screen has the added option of allowing the user to sort results by hit frequency, date, author, or title.

SPECIALIZED SEARCH ENGINES

The Web offers many specialized search engines that tap Invisible Web content. The role of specialized search engines is to dig more deeply into a subject area than might be expected from general-purpose search engines. The latter are sometimes described as doing "horizontal searching," that is, searching for information on a topic broadly across many kinds of resources. Specialized search engines offer "vertical searching," more focused searching in resources that concentrate on specific topics. Specialization leads them to delve deeper into Invisible Web resources and offer their users more complete results. Figure 6-8 illustrates the differences between horizontal and vertical searching. For those looking for a very narrow specialization, there are also "niche" search tools. The progressive use of these tools is demonstrated by a search for science information. The researcher begins with a general-purpose search engine, progresses to a specialized search engine that concentrates, say, on biology, and finally looks for a niche resource that focuses, perhaps, on microbiology. The more specialized the tool, the less need for screening out irrelevant results. Figure 6-8 shows how horizontal, vertical, and niche tools relate.

▶ FIGURE 6-8: Horizontal, Vertical, and Niche Tools Relationship

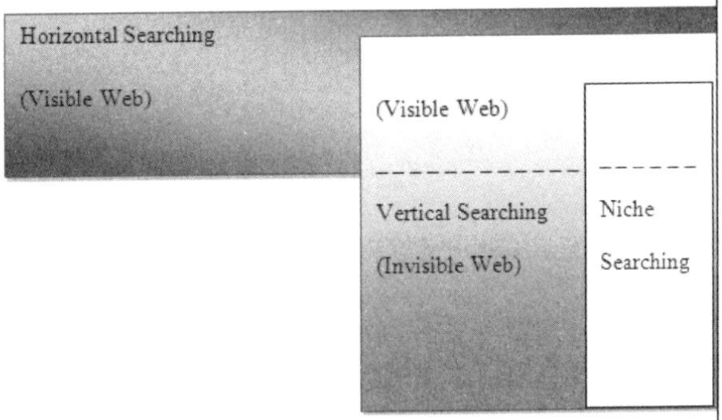

Horizontal Searching

(Visible Web)

(Visible Web)

Vertical Searching

(Invisible Web)

Niche Searching

Invisible Web Search Engines

Few attempts have been made to create Invisible Web search engines and only a few have survived.

CompletePlanet: The Deep Web Directory (www.completeplanet.com)

CompletePlanet was developed in 2000 and offers a keyword search feature along with a directory of resources. CompletePlanet includes in its resources more than 70,000 databases and specialty search engines. CompletePlanet was developed by BrightPlanet, the organization that sponsored a famous "white paper" on the Invisible Web that gave researchers an idea of the content and possibilities of the Invisible Web (Bergman, 2001). Recognizing that the Invisible Web is heavily composed of database content, CompletePlanet was created to help locate those databases. Researchers must still enter the databases and query them utilizing the individual search features of each database.

IncyWincy: The Invisible Web Search Engine (www.incywincy.com)

IncyWincy, another early tool, also investigates the need for the researcher to enter databases to retrieve content. It relates to the Invisible Web by providing a "Form" search option. The search results include a search form for each database. The user can fill in the search forms in the IncyWincy results list and connect quickly to the results of various databases. This process streamlines research by saving the step of connecting first to the database and then entering a query. Both CompletePlanet and IncyWincy are only superficially Invisible Web tools. General-purpose search engines can also find databases and bring users to database search features.

Turbo10: Search the Deep Net (http://turbo10.com)

Turbo10 is a more recent approach to Invisible Web research. Turbo10 claims to be a metasearch tool that accesses both surface and more specialized or vertical search engines. By including some vertical search engines in its results list, it can claim Invisible Web capability. Users must judge its overall effectiveness for their needs.

All these tools have limitations. The real growth area in Invisible Web searching is in the development of vertical search engines.

Vertical Search Engines

The principal characteristic of a vertical search tool is its concentration in a specific subject area. Because of its focus, it will look extensively for resources wherever placed on the Web. Users of vertical search engines can expect to find results designed to meet their needs. Thomas Pack, writing for *Online*, states that vertical search tools "are distinguished not by how much information they give you but by

---

▶FIGURE 6-9: Scirus (http://scirus.com)

SCIrUS
for scientific information only

Advanced search | Preferences

[   ] [Search]

SCIrUS is the most comprehensive scientific research tool on the web. With over 450 million scientific items indexed at last count, it allows researchers to search for not only journal content but also scientists' homepages, courseware, pre-print server material, patents and institutional repository and website information.

Scirus Topics Pages [Beta] now online...

Latest Scientific News - from New Scientist

Source: Reprinted with permission of Scirus.

---

how little, favoring precision over recall, and that's the primary benefit they offer. Vertical search tools can often save you time because you don't have to weed out as much irrelevant information as you would with a general search engine" (Pack, 2001: 44). Examples of vertical search engines in science follow.

Scirus for Scientific Information Only (http://scirus.com)

Scirus searches more than 450 million science-specific Web resources, among them articles, patents, and journals that general-purpose search engines overlook (see Figure 6-9). It seeks out Invisible Web materials and, according to its own description, "goes deeper than the first two levels of a Web site, thereby revealing much more relevant information" (http://scirus.com/srsapp/aboutus/).

A search on the topic of "global warming" produces more than a million results, but the Scirus results screen can also help the user filter the results by type of sources. The user can further refine the search by linking through related subtopics such as "greenhouse gas emissions" that can be turned into new searches. Not all results lead to full text, especially of journal articles; however, information about which subscription database offers the journal in full text is provided.

Science.gov (www.science.gov)

Science.gov (see Figure 6-10) is a federally sponsored search engine for government science information. Redesigned in September 2008, it provides resources from 36 databases, more than 1,850 Web sites, and is intended for the use of professionals, students, teachers, and the business community. For those looking for any science-related information, it provides a wealth of authoritative materials.

Searching for "global warming" in Science.gov returns over 2,000 results, all linked to full text. The government agency source is listed in each result. Science.gov utilizes Explorit, a technology developed by the Deep Web Technologies Company. As the

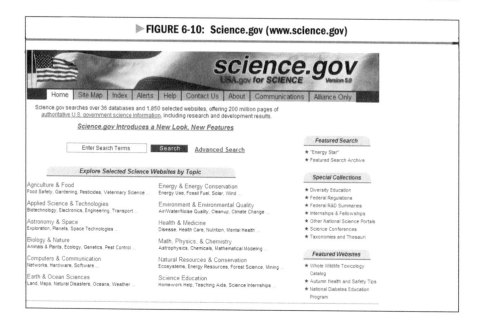

▶ FIGURE 6-10: Science.gov (www.science.gov)

screenshot of the Science.gov homepage shows, the site can also be used as a directory. By choosing a subject, the user can obtain results that include a list of narrower topics as well as a list of databases and Web sites. Science.gov also does "real-time" searching. General-purpose search engines connect users to prepackaged results screens, and therefore can provide quick response time for a search, but less than current results. Real-time searching, on the other hand, compiles the results at the time of the query and the results are always completely up-to-date. As Science.gov is a specialized search engine and searches only government science resources, it can offer real-time searching without the searches taking excessive time to complete.

ScienceResearch.com (www.scienceresearch.com)

Sponsored by Deep Web Technologies, ScienceResearch.com is a freely accessible search engine offering resources that include journals and public science databases (see Figure 6-11). Launched in 2005, it is intended for students, teachers, and researchers. A ScienceResearch.com search for "global warming" returned 25 results. Included in each result is the source of the documents. The source materials themselves are not available in full text within ScienceResearch. com, but the search engine connects the user to the publishing agencies. ScienceResearch.com also utilizes real-time searching and displays a graphic while compiling the results to show the progress. ScienceResearch.com also offers a directory approach from its homepage with a list of scientific disciplines. Choosing a category leads to a list of databases and Web sites.

▷ **FIGURE 6-11: ScienceResearch.com (www.scienceresearch.com)**

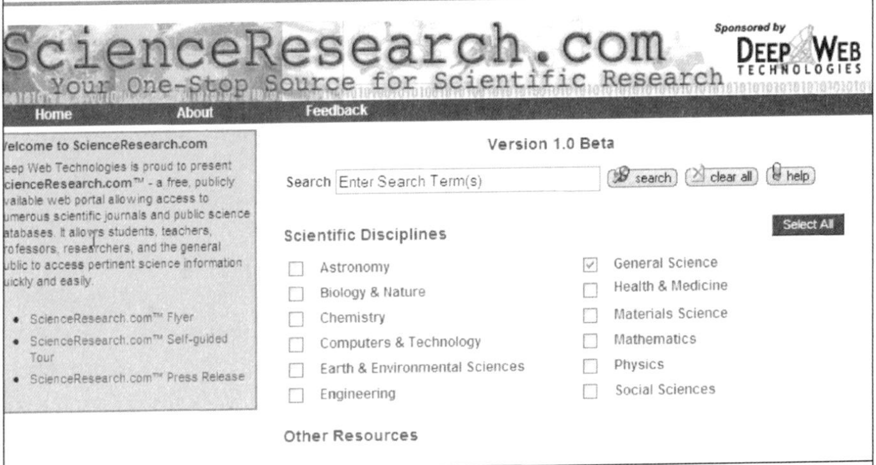

Source: Reprinted with permission of Deep Web Technologies.

These three science-related vertical search engines cover some of the same sources but each also captures different resources. ScienceResearch.com, for instance, offers a subject category on the social sciences, a subject area not included in Scirus.com or Science.gov. Scirus.com includes features on current news items, which are not offered by other search engines. Science.gov focuses only on government research but always gives links to full-text that the others do not provide. Users can decide which vertical search engine best suits their needs.

Niche Search Engines

Niche search engines are even more specialized than vertical search engines. They may appeal to a limited audience but can help those users by providing the very specific kinds of information important to them.

FurnitureStyleSearch.com (http://furniturestylesearch.com)

An example of a niche product is FurnitureStyleSearch.com (http://furniturestylesearch.com), intended for both consumers as well as industry people. Users can find out about retailers, furniture models, related terms, and much more, but the intent and scope is very focused.

GuideStar (www.guidestar.org)

GuideStar (www.guidestar.org) can help consumers research and donate to charitable organizations.

Technorati (http://technorati.com)

Another example is Technorati (http://technorati.com), which searches only blogs and other forms of tagged social media. Niche search engines are available for almost any need and can be found easily on the Web.

Semantic Web Search Engines

The Semantic Web idea is the creation of Tim Berners-Lee, inventor of the World Wide Web (Berners-Lee, Hendler, and Lassila, 2001). Semantic Web searching will recognize the context for which a user is creating a search. Results will be identified by recognizing the ideas found within the resources rather than just by matching keywords. Although the Semantic Web approach has been much discussed, few practical examples are available. Much of the discussion involves the technical aspects of making it work. Hakia.com is a working example of this new approach.

hakia (http://www.hakia.com)

hakia.com is in beta testing (see Figure 6-12). A search for "global warming" produces results organized by various approaches such as "scientific evidence" or "data and statistics." The categories give users the opportunity to select the more specific type of material that they need.

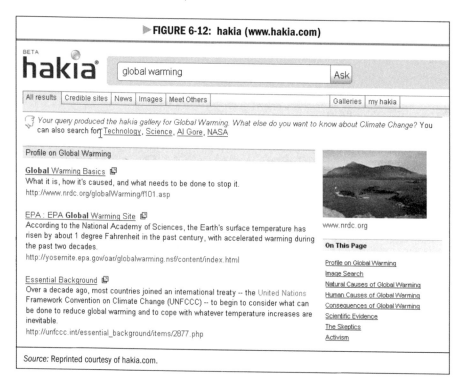

▶ **FIGURE 6-12: hakia (www.hakia.com)**

Source: Reprinted courtesy of hakia.com.

▶ TABLE 6-1: Summary of Internet Research Tools			
Types of Tools	When a Researcher Needs . . .	Invisible Web or Surface Web	Examples
Directories	▶ a broad overview of topics ▶ a hierarchical arrangement of subject ▶ individually reviewed resources ▶ quality Web site results	Hybrid tools covering the best of both worlds	Librarians Internet Index Open Directory Project INFOMINE
Databases (free and subscription)	▶ subject specialization and clearly defined content ▶ dynamically generated results ▶ currency ▶ searching by fields	Invisible Web	Thomas LexisNexis Academic (subscription) Hoover's Business & Company Resource Center (subscription) ERIC
Specialized Search Engines (vertical and niche)	▶ specialized coverage of topics and disciplines (e.g., science, medicine, etc.) ▶ real-time searching	Hybrid tools	Scirus.com Science.gov ScienceResearch.com hakia.com

CONCLUSIONS

As this review illustrates, many types of tools can help students with their research. Learning about these tools and when to use them should be part of information literacy education. Table 6-1 summarizes the tools reviewed in the chapter.

REFERENCES

Bergman, Michael K. 2001. "The deep Web: Surfacing hidden value." White paper. Bright-Planet. Available: http://www.brightplanet.com/images/stories/pdf/deepwebwhitepaper.pdf (accessed October 9, 2008).

Berners-Lee, Tim, James Hendler, and Ora Lassila. 2001. "The semantic Web." *Scientific American* (May). Available: http://ebscohost.com/ (accessed October 9, 2008).

Pack, Thomas. 2001. "Getting vertical to cut research time." *Online* 25, no.5: 44–48.

►Part III

NARROWING THE GAP BETWEEN THE VISIBLE AND INVISIBLE WEB

7

VISIBLE VERSUS INVISIBLE WEB: SHIFTING BOUNDARIES

INTRODUCTION

Since the coinage of the phrase "Invisible Web" by Dr. Jill Ellsworth in 1994 (Bergman, 2001), a whole industry has been at work on various levels to narrow the gap between the "surface" or "visible" Web and the "deep," "hidden," "dark," "cloaked," or "invisible" Web. In the commercial world, Google is spending millions of dollars on projects such as Google Scholar and Google Book Search. It seems that there are almost daily announcements of new search engines aimed at tapping Invisible Web content (see Chapter 6): Turbo10 and CloserLook Search. Companies such as Deep Web Technologies power databases as varied as ScienceResearch.com and Science.gov. New noncommercial initiatives such as the Open Content Alliance, OCLC's WorldCat, and the Open Archives Initiatives (2002) are taking root in the information world. Library professionals are re-creating their online public catalogs to make them more user friendly for today's students at North Carolina State University, Plymouth State University, and Georgia Public Libraries, while integrated library system (ILS) companies are developing next-generation interfaces with new catalog overlay software products such as Primo, Encore, and AquaBrowser.

This chapter addresses the phenomenon of the shifting boundaries between the visible and the Invisible Web. It highlights some trends in the information world, whether in the commercial or the nonprofit sector, but it does not pretend to cover an all-inclusive list of new technologies. Even as this chapter is being written, information professionals are experimenting with new solutions to the problem of Invisible Web access.

RELATIVE SIZE OF THE SURFACE WEB AND THE INVISIBLE WEB

Statistical information about the depth of the Invisible or deep Web has multiplied since 2001, when Michael K. Bergman wrote in his seminal white paper titled "The Deep Web: Surfacing Hidden Value" that the Invisible Web was 400 to 550 times larger than the surface Web (Bergman, 2001: 1). In 2003, the School of Information Management and Systems at the University of California, Berkeley, published a document titled "How Much Information 2003" (see Figure 7-1) in which the size of the 2002 Internet, given in terabytes, included the "Surface Web" (167 terabytes), the "Deep Web" (91,850), "E-mail (originals)" (440,606) and "Instant messaging" (274) (Lyman and Varian, 2003).

In "What's Next for Google," an article published in the January 2005 issue of *Technology Review,* Charles H. Ferguson created a table to compare the deep Web to various other forms of digital media, using the statistics from "How Much Information? 2003" mentioned previously (Ferguson, 2005: 41).

In a Web document titled "What Is 'The Invisible Web'?" posted on About.com, Paul Gil offers the following statistics, current to Fall 2007:

▶ Google.com indexes 12.5 billion public Web pages.
▶ 71 billion static web pages are publicly available on the World Wide Web.
▶ 6.5 billion static pages are hidden from the public.
▶ 220+ billion database-driven pages are invisible to Google. (Gil, 2008)

The same document links to a Summer 2005 diagram of the World Wide Web as seen in four layers (see Figure 7-2). Layer 3 (dynamic database content such as EBSCOhost or LexisNexis) and Layer 4 (completely private Web sites with dynamic content, paid memberships, company intranets, or private extranets, such as nytimes.com) form the Invisible Web and are by far the largest components of the Web (Illustration of the World Wide Web, 2005).

▶ **FIGURE 7-1: How Much Information 2003**

Table 1.13: The size of the Internet in terabytes.

Medium	2002 Terabytes
Surface Web	167
Deep Web	91,850
Email (originals)	440,606
Instant messaging	274
TOTAL	532,897

Source: How much information 2003

Source: From "How Much Information 2003," School of Information, UC Berkeley.

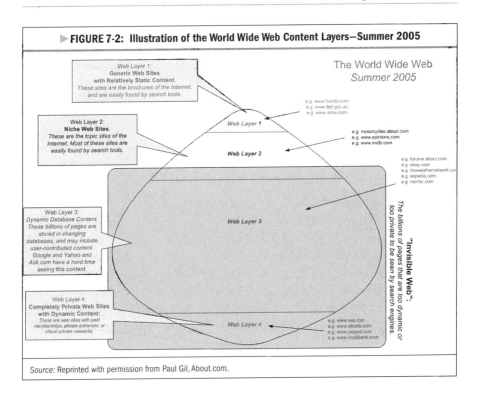

▷FIGURE 7-2: Illustration of the World Wide Web Content Layers—Summer 2005

Source: Reprinted with permission from Paul Gil, About.com.

These graphics illustrate two points: (1) the continued preoccupation of information professionals with the uncovering of the Invisible Web and (2) the mainstreaming of the concept.

Statistics are one way to depict the gap between the visible and Invisible Web in learning and teaching. Faculty explaining to students the research required for their courses can use these statistics to focus on the fact that research on the Internet must include content from the Invisible Web, databases being the primary example in this category. The graphics reinforce the concept that using general-purpose search engines would give a student only a tiny fraction of the wealth of information actually available on the Web.

COMMERCIAL GENERAL-PURPOSE SEARCH ENGINE INROADS INTO THE INVISIBLE WEB

One of the ways in which commercial giants such as Google and Yahoo! continue their dominance of the Web is by rolling out new products to narrow the gap between the visible and the Invisible Web.

Google Scholar

On its "About Google Scholar" page, Google Scholar explains that it

> provides a simple way to broadly search for scholarly literature. From one place, you can search across many disciplines and sources: peer-reviewed papers, theses, books, abstracts and articles, from academic publishers, professional societies, preprint repositories, universities and other scholarly organizations. Google Scholar helps you identify the most relevant research across the world of scholarly research. (Google Scholar, 2008)

This inroad by Google into the scholarly realm will definitely uncover a large portion of the Invisible Web and transfer it to the surface Web. It will be popular with students and faculty because one search will uncover articles from myriad sources.

Whether Google Scholar should always be the place for academics to start their research remains to be seen and is hotly debated in the library world. Librarians and other information professionals are wondering what Google considers "scholarly." The company is silent on this issue for the time being. Furthermore, when a search is performed in Google Scholar, the results retrieved vary from citations to book previews to abstracts to full-text subscription databases. The analysis of such uneven results could provide an opportunity for teaching faculty and librarians to introduce information literacy and critical thinking skills into the curriculum. An interesting class discussion could center on the pros and cons of using Google Scholar as a tool for research.

Google Book Search

Another controversial innovation by Google is its Book Search, first named Google Print, which has two components. The Google Books Library Project partners with libraries (Google Book Search, 2008) and the Google Book Partners Program is the commercial branch wherein authors and publishers can have their books promoted by Google. Google Book Search offers access in varying degrees (full view, preview, snippet) to books from publishers and libraries through the Google interface. For the Books Library Project, Google initially contracted with five major research libraries (Stanford, New York Public Research Library, Michigan, Oxford, and Harvard) to scan their entire collections (Albacete, 2005). However, the company met stiff opposition from publishers and librarians regarding the digitization of material still under copyright, and in 2005, the Authors' Guild and the Association of American Publishers sued Google for infringement of copyright (Young, 2005; Carlson, 2005). Information professionals argue that, even if Google provides only a digitized snippet of a copyrighted book, as it advertises on the Books Library Project homepage, it has scanned the entire text and therefore that text is stored digitally somewhere under Google's control. If a library allows the mass digitization of its collections, Google holds books under copyright in digital format, potentially negating the rights of authors and publishers. However, more and more libraries are signing on, as is evident on the homepage of the project (Google Books Library Project, 2008). Whatever the outcome of this new initiative, Google's digitization of books goes a long way toward making "visible" material that was heretofore unavailable to the public. The book becomes part of the visible Web, narrowing once again the gap between the surface and the deep Web. Even if users see only a snippet of a chapter, they can use the information accessed as is or turn to an academic institution and find the book itself to continue the research. As Karen Coyle concludes, "Google has clearly stated that their book project is solely aimed at providing a searchable index to the books on library shelves" (Coyle, 2006: 644).

Crawling through HTML Forms

In April 2008, two members of the Google Crawling and Indexing Team announced that Google had begun indexing dynamically generated Web pages, that is, crawling through data heretofore inaccessible that was part of the Invisible or deep Web. The giant search engine company has been experimenting with the ability to access information by using their spider software to fill out HTML forms. It claims that it will be able to crawl through sources found through drop-down menus and dynamically generated pages. In a comment posted to the Official Google Webmaster Central Blog on April 11, 2008, Jayant Madhavan and Alon Halen noted that "[b]y crawling using HTML forms (and abiding by robots.txt), we are able to lead search engine users to documents that would otherwise not be easily found in search engines, and provide webmasters and users alike with a better and more comprehensive search experience." This represents an enormous technological breakthrough in the indexing of sources found in publicly accessible databases.

Yahoo! Initiatives

In June 2005, Yahoo! rolled out Yahoo Search Subscriptions to tap deep Web subscription content from fee-based databases such as LexisNexis, Consumer Reports, the Financial Times, Factiva, Forrester Online, the New England Journal of Medicine, the Wall Street Journal (30 days), TheStreet.com, and IEEE publications. Yahoo! proposed to index some of the material on these sites and include them in the Yahoo! search capability (Price, 2005). However, in order to access the actual content, the user would still need a subscription to each database. For students, such access is usually not a problem, but for the general public, it may be. This Yahoo!

service taps Invisible Web sources hidden in subscription databases, collections of material tailor-made for students. As of June 2008, Yahoo! Search Subscriptions still seems to be in beta testing (Yahoo! Search Subscriptions, 2008). In his November 2005 column in *Information Today*, Mick O'Leary wrote a scathing critique of this Yahoo! product. He argued that the search interface is quite limited, that it is hard to find Yahoo! Search Subscriptions because it is separate from the main Yahoo! search site, and that the databases it proposes to search are not very deep (O'Leary, 2005: 39–43).

In 2004, Yahoo! Search launched its new Content Acquisition Program (CAP) to allow commercial and noncommercial providers to add their content to the Yahoo! Search index. Public Site Match, the noncommercial component of the Content Acquisition Program, makes inroads into the deep Web by adding material from content providers such as National Public Radio, the Library of Congress, and Northwestern University's online OYEZ project of Supreme Court audio recordings since 1995. Other partners include the New York Public Library, Project Gutenberg, University of Michigan's OAIster project, UCLA's Cuneiform Digital Library Initiative, Wikipedia, and National Science Digital Library (Yahoo!, 2004). This initiative allows searchers to obtain data from these providers through Yahoo! Search, once again moving Invisible Web content to the visible surface. As of June 2008, this initiative is not very successful.

OCLC

There have also been various partnerships between OCLC and Yahoo! as well as between OCLC and Google. In December 2003, OCLC announced that it would make available information from WorldCat through the Google and Yahoo! search interfaces. A Yahoo! search on "how to talk to kids so they will listen" yielded, in June 2008, a twenty-seventh entry for "Find in a library: How to talk so kids will listen" with the URL "worldcatlibraries.org." The nearest library that owns the book can be located by zip code, state, province, or country. Interestingly enough, the same search in Google did not bring up the WorldCat link in the first ten pages. "The goal of the pilot is to make libraries more visible to Web users and more accessible from the sites where many people begin to look for information" (O'Neill, 2004: 54).

Deep Web Search Engines

Every day a new search engine claims to outdo all the other search engines people use on a daily basis. This section can only scratch the surface and highlight a few unusual search engines that claim to tap Invisible Web content.

One of the newer kids on the block is the search engine enth.com (http://enth.com/), which claims to "create new content in response to a search request" (Enth.com, 2008). The ability to access not just Web pages but content in databases is intriguing: Enth has the ability to transform a question from a user into language that databases understand (Hall, 2007: 9), but the coverage of this search engine is presently restricted to sports. KoolTorch (http://kooltorch.com/) presents all results in a graphical user interface (GUI) and uses a "taxonomy overlay" (Smith, 2007), whereby groups with common traits are displayed in circular icons.

Vertical Search Engines

General-purpose search engines find information horizontally, across the expanse of Web content. Using specialized search engines that concentrate on one subject area, be it science, government, or medicine, is called vertical searching. Instead of doing a Google search that will pull up an overwhelming number of results, it often behooves a user to try a vertical search engine specializing in the content area desired. To look up information on a government branch, use usa.gov (http://www.usa.gov/); for scientific information, try usa.gov for science (http://science.gov/), or Scirus (http://scirus.com/) (see Chapter 6 for further analysis); for medical information, WebMD. Some companies will provide vertical searching for a fee; for example, Deep Web Technologies provides federated searching across various databases in the fields of science and technology, offering results lists without duplicates, ranked in accordance with the needs of the customer (http://www.deepwebtech.com/). CloserLook Search (http://www.closerlooksearch.com) offers specialized searching in fields such as health, travel, and business, and offers to perform searches in the deep Web. One can obtain company profiles or business background information in real time for a fee.

Microsoft

Microsoft announced in 2005 that it would digitize approximately 100,000 out-of-copyright books from the British Library (Guth, 2005). This partnership ended in May 2008, although the British Library is continuing the digitization project on its own (Kirk, 2008).

Microsoft is also financing in part the Internet Archive, a nonprofit organization dedicated to preserving historical collections in digital format (Internet Archive, 2008). It is using the Internet Archive for the digitization program of out-of-copyright library materials through the Open Content Alliance, a permanent archive of digitized collections from a variety of organizations around the world (see also p. 122).

ProQuest DigitalCommons@

ProQuest/UMI began offering a new service in 2004 known as DigitalCommons@, a digital institutional repository service (Orphan, 2004). It provides software to research institutions to help digitize and make accessible local materials such as dissertations, unpublished manuscripts, and open access material. Digital Commons@ is another initiative that brings material to the Web through general-purpose search engines—material heretofore available only to the home institution. Berkeley Electronic Press announced in summer 2006 that it will purchase this turnkey institutional repository software from ProQuest.

Web 2.0

Web 2.0 is a term for newer forms of technology including blogs, social bookmarking, RSS feeds, wikis, and podcasts. The common element of these new tools is the ability to customize and share information. More and more blogs appear in general-purpose search engines and this tendency will increase with mergers such as the purchase of Blogger by Google. It is probably just a matter of time before most blogs will be indexed by search engines. Social bookmarking sites such as Delicious (http://delicious/), Furl (http://furl.net/), or CiteULike (http://www.citeulike.org/) allow users to save favorite sites from within the visible or the Invisible Web and make them available to their "friends." Although presently not picked up by general-purpose search engines, some "favorites" from social bookmarking sites are crossing the boundary from Invisible to "visible to a few." Information within wikis, the most famous of which is Wikipedia, can be found on the visible Web unless the wiki is password-protected. Some of these new technological ventures allow the possibility of using Invisible Web content and bringing it into an online social forum where it can be accessed by other users of that forum.

All these commercial ventures are still in their infancy and it is too early to judge their full impact on searching capabilities for the public. As most Invisible Web material resides in databases, all of these initiatives undertaken by commercial general-purpose search engines are chipping away and penetrating databases, offering searchers ever-increasing access to information formerly hidden from public view.

INITIATIVES TO NARROW THE GAP BETWEEN VISIBLE AND INVISIBLE WEB

At the same time as commercial entities are making more Invisible Web content retrievable through their search engines, thereby narrowing the gap between the deep and the surface Web, the opposite tendency is also at work. This section shows how librarians and other information professionals are tweaking access to material in proprietary databases, especially library catalogs. The purpose is to make it easier for students to search—whether by refining the search interface or by expanding the breadth of sources available through one search. Again, the result is to reduce the gap between searches in general-purpose search engines and those in library catalogs and databases.

Next-generation Library Catalogs

Next-generation library catalogs are being implemented, some by librarians in conjunction with their parent institutions, others by nonprofit organizations or commercial integrated library system (ILS) vendors. These newer library interfaces, whether tacked onto an existing online public access catalog (OPAC) or slowly replacing it, do not change the balance between the visible and the Invisible Web per se. Most of them, however, do mirror the search interfaces of Google and Amazon.com interfaces that students are quite familiar with. The capabilities of these next-generation OPACs, or "discovery tools" as they are often called nowadays, should have the beneficial effect of drawing students toward the library interface by offering them a research environment that they have become comfortable using. The ideal would be to provide seamless Web access to library catalogs, thereby blurring the lines between "visible" and "invisible" and giving students the ability to find sources through a single interface. This scenario remains a dream at the moment, but the various innovations being undertaken to provide adequate resources to students represent steps toward that ideal.

One of the better examples of new technology that enhances an OPAC is Endeca's Information Access Platform software, used to add functionality to the catalog of the North Carolina State University Libraries (NCSUL) (http://www.lib.nscu.edu/catalog). Prior to January 2006, when NCSU implemented Endeca, it had been limited to use in the business world. The enhancements offered include relevance-ranked results, faceted navigation (shortcuts to narrowing search results) and new browsing features (the ability to browse without entering a query). A search can be divided by collection, topic, genre, format, region, era, or language. Clicking on a title gives the option to look at the table of contents, browse by call number through all the titles in that classification, or look at "more titles like this" or "more by these authors." The guided navigation operates both at the bibliographic record level and at the item level enabling users to browse by format, availability, or "new book" and also by all the elements in a Machine Readable Cataloging (MARC) record. Endeca software also allows automatic spell correction through the message "Did you mean . . ." (Antelman, Lynema, and Pace, 2006: 130). The NCSUL catalog mirrors in many ways the speed and convenience of a general-purpose search engine, luring students to vetted sources through a Google-like interface (Jacso, 2007). As students are accustomed to some these features from commercial Web sites such as Amazon.com or Barnesandnoble.com, "more titles like this" features have been very popular (Antelman, Lyneman, and Pace, 2006: 134). It must be stressed again that this next-generation catalog still requires a student to make a separate search in an Invisible Web tool. But the familiarity of some of the search features make an OPAC such as NCSUL's more inviting to today's students. Thus, Amanda, the hypothetical student of Chapter 5, should have no more trouble navigating an OPAC such as NCSUL's than she does a general-purpose search engine such as Google.

Similar projects to enhance OPACs exist in various institutions, whether public or academic, with some differences. All aim, if not to narrow the gap between the "visible" and the "invisible" Web, then at least to meet student expectations of searching with a more Google-like interface.

The Research Libraries Group's (RLG) RedLightGreen project ran from fall 2003 until November 2006 when RLG was absorbed into OCLC. It was an initiative directed at making searching easier for students by offering alternative search options. In RedLightGreen, a topic could be further subdivided by subject, author, or language. The application of a FRBR (Functional Requirements for Bibliographic Records) approach in the RedLightGreen project allowed all editions of a work to be linked together instead of remaining in separate records, as is the case in most Machine Readable Cataloging (MARC)–based catalogs. Although now defunct, this prototype of a new kind of library database showed the potential for making library resources easier for students to search and use.

At Plymouth State University Lamson Library, a front-end to the library catalog was developed using open source WordPress blog management software (Jacso, 2007: 56). This catalog (www.plymouth.edu/library) offers features similar to those of the catalog at North Carolina State University: topics can be browsed by subject, author, and media format. Each catalog record contains cover pages, book reviews, tables of contents, and various other services. Jenny Levine noted in the ALA TechSource Blog posted on January 20, 2006, that every record has its own page with a static link, therefore indexable by general-purpose search engines. The OPAC is now powered by Scriblio, a free open-source content management system based on WordPress (http://about.scriblio.net).

Another OPAC enhancement is AquaBrowser in use at the Queens Library (http://aqua.queenslibrary.org/) in New York. "The product provides libraries with a way to supplement or replace their existing catalog with one that includes faceted navigation, relevance ranking, visual search, and other features in high demand today" (Breeding, 2007: 15). A "Word Cloud Search" offers, in a graphical interface, a list of related keywords connected by spokes to the original search term. When the user clicks on any one of the related terms, that keyword becomes the central figure in the cloud and all the titles associated with the term are listed. With Web 2.0 technology allowing users to tag their sites in social bookmarking software, this "word cloud" in an OPAC is a research feature that parallels what students are using, again making the library environment more user-friendly.

Other next-generation OPACs with many of the features outlined above include Primo, an Ex-Libris product, exemplified by the tag line "Find It, Get It" (Breeding, 2007: 28), and Encore, known as a "discovery services platform," a product of Innovative Interfaces. An in-house system, Evergreen, was developed at Georgia Public Library (http://gapines.org/opac/en-US/skin/default/xml/index.xml) for the Georgia PINES consortium.

A project is under way at the University of Rochester River Campus Libraries to develop a new interface to their online catalog called the eXtensible Catalog, using XC code, "to provide open source applications to simplify user access to all library resources, digital and non-digital." It will offer many Web 2.0 functionalities including blogs, wikis, RSS feeds, and folksonomies. The goal is to "[b]uild a suite of open-source applications for libraries to reveal their collections on the web" (University of Rochester, 2008). A second aim is to provide access to all the resources through one interface, thereby "eliminating the data silos that are now likely to exist between a library's OPAC and its various digital repositories and commercial databases" (Bowen, 2008: 8). This project is entering its second phase which will last until 2009.

In April 2007, OCLC launched an online public catalog with the University of Washington (http://uwashington.worldcat.org/) as part of a pilot project (Breeding, 2007: 33). WorldCat is a known entity in the library world. It entered the public domain with its online version, WorldCat.org, launched in 2006, followed now with an integrated library system. WorldCat Local works contrary to usual online catalogs in which a search is limited to the library's collections; World-Cat Local provides a user access to the entire WorldCat bibliographic database as well as to the local collection. What is especially appealing in the WorldCat Local interface is the availability of article citations mixed in with book and Internet resources in the results list.

Federated Searching

Federated searching, "also known as parallel search, metasearch, or broadcast search" (Fyer, 2004: 16), is another method for the information industry to present users with simpler interfaces to search various databases simultaneously. "Some librarians believe that metasearch could be a way to meet the expectations and needs of 'the Google generation'" (Luther, 2003: 36). In effect, federated searching creates a portal that allows searching across the various library platforms using a single search box, "à la Google." E-collections, OPACs, subscription databases, digital institutional repositories, and the Web can be combined into one search interface. Developing the capability for federated searching is a slow and arduous process involving difficult decisions regarding the customization of the user interface, authentication for remote access, and the organization of data from various databases, a very labor-intensive and expensive endeavor. As Donna Fyer points out in her article, "Federated Search Engines" (Fyer, 2004: 16–19), there is a difference between metasearch engines that search a topic across multiple Web search engines at once and federated searches that search Invisible Web content such as library subscription databases and locally created digital content by performing the search in each database. "Federated search offers another opportunity for libraries to out-Google Google, this time by returning relevant results that Google misses" (Fyer, 2004: 18).

Indexing the Invisible Web

The race is on, on various fronts, toward the indexing of the Invisible Web. Yanbo Ru and Ellis Horowitz summarize these developments in their article, "Indexing the Invisible Web: A Survey" (Ru and Horowitz, 2005). However, they caution that "[s]imply indexing the search interface of an invisible web site is insufficient. There may be content within the web site that users are unable to discover" (Ru and Horowitz, 2005: 261).

Other Noncommercial Initiatives

These initiatives continue the trend to make content heretofore Invisible available through various interfaces, not necessarily through general-purpose search engines but through individual searchable Web sites. Students, as has been shown in various previous chapters, must be redirected to use these alternative sites when appropriate.

Open Content Alliance (OCA)

The Open Content Alliance was born as a reaction to Google's Books Search Program. It distinguishes itself from Google in three ways: (1) it will digitize only books in the public domain, (2) it will make its technology public, and (3) it is a library-driven initiative with the scanning done by the Internet Archive (Coyle, 2006: 641–642). The Internet Archive is an organization dedicated to the preservation of Web sites and is best known for its Wayback Machine, which archives Web sites since the mid-1990s (Bengston, 2006: 3). Although OCA is a nonprofit organization, it receives funding from commercial giants such as Microsoft, Yahoo!, Adobe, and others. Yahoo! will supply the search engine for the scanned books of the OCA. The digitized books will be available for downloading and printing since all the material digitized is out of copyright (Tennant, 2005). The OCA is preserving not only books but also PDFs (Portable Document Format) and JPEGs (Joint Photographic Experts Group), and other raw camera images (Bengston, 2006: 3).

Open Archives Initiative (OAI)

The Open Archives Initiative was launched in 2001 with the mission to "develop and promote interoperability standards that aim to facilitate the efficient dissemination of content" (Shreeves et al., 2005: 577). It developed a protocol for exchanging metadata (OAI-PMH) based on the Simple Dublin Core format, a tool to catalog various types of objects not limited to books. The idea is to standardize the metadata to allow greater access and visibility to hidden resources (Cole et al., 2002). Heretofore, these resources have not been well indexed by general-purpose search engines. This protocol is slowly being adopted by various institutions and allows "federated access to dispersed resources" (Shreeves et al., 2005: 578). Again, this development brings Invisible Web content to light: By making metadata openly available, OAI greatly enhances access to Web material, once again reducing the gap between the visible and the Invisible Web.

Project Gutenberg

In 1971, Michael Hart started this initiative, the goal of which is to provide "a free public library of 10,000 public-domain electronic books" (Hane, 2004: 28), available at www. gutenberg.org/wiki/Main_Page. That goal was reached in October 2003. Hart now wants to digitize 10 million books (Hane, 2004: 52). Presently, the collection consists of approximately 25,000 titles that are either out of copyright (published before 1923) or for which an author has turned over the copyright to the public. The site is run by volunteers who apparently choose which books to digitize. The most popular titles downloaded include Shakespeare, Mark Twain, and Sir Arthur Conan Doyle (Fisher, 2006).

The Semantic Web

Tim Berners-Lee, who is credited with inventing the World Wide Web in the late 1980s, now heads the World Web Consortium, which is working on the Semantic Web. The Semantic Web is defined as "a visionary project that aims to enhance the usability and usefulness of the Web by enabling computers to find, read, understand, and use the content of Web documents to accomplish tasks via automated agents and Web-based services" (Kay, 2006: 32). This new initiative is also called Web 3.0. The structure to be imposed on Web pages by the Semantic Web falls between the unstructured free text of the Web and the highly structured information found in databases (Ding et al., 2005: 62). Tagging elements of information within Web documents will eventually allow software to locate information within Web pages that will once again make more sources visible to users. "In one sense, the Semantic Web will become a kind of global database" (Kay, 2006: 32). One example of a semantic search engine, hakia, is still in beta testing. (See Chapter 6 for more information.)

CONCLUSIONS

The continued emphasis in the information industry on the unavailability of Invisible Web content to general-purpose search engines has had the positive effect of furthering research, fueled primarily by commercial competition, to bring as much Web content as possible to light through common interfaces. The competition between Google and the library sector aims at the healthy, common goal of moving more and more Invisible Web material into the surface Web. All of these endeavors, whether commercial or nonprofit, vendor or library initiated, chip away at the Invisible Web by bringing sources to the surface. In many cases, material from databases, which represents the bulk of the Invisible Web, gets picked up by search engines and made readily available to students. However, the Invisible Web is also growing exponentially and remains an unmanageable entity. In his book *Google Power*, Chris Sherman quotes a Google chief technology officer who said that "it would take Google engineers 50 years to fully crack the invisible Web problem" (Sherman, 2005: 17). Despite all the efforts of the various initiatives touched upon in this chapter, both parts of the Web, the surface and the deep, are far from being readily accessible to users, especially to students doing research. Intermediaries, whether faculty or librarians, must play a role in presenting students with a full portrait of the information world as it is today.

REFERENCES

Albacete, Andrew. 2005. "Google to digitize 15 million books." *Library Journal* (January): 18–22. Available: http://web.ebscohost.com (accessed October 9, 2008).

Antelman, Kristin, Emily Lynema, and Andrew K. Pace. 2006. "Toward a twenty-first century library catalog." *Information Technology and Libraries* (September): 128–139. Available: http://web.ebscohost.com (accessed October 9, 2008).

Bengston, Jonathan B. 2006. "The birth of the universal library." *Netconnect* (Spring): 2–6. Available: http://web.ebscohost.com (accessed October 9, 2008).

Bergman, Michael K. 2001. "The deep Web: Surfacing hidden value." White paper. Bright-Planet. Available: www.brightplanet.com/images/stories/pdf/deepwebwhitepaper.pdf (accessed December 9, 2008).

Bowen, Jennifer. 2008. "Metadata to support next-generation library resource discovery: Lessons from the eXtensible Catalog, phase 1." *Information Technology and Libraries* (June): 6–19. Available: https://urresearch.rochester.edu/handle/1802/5757 (accessed December 7, 2008).

Breeding, Marshall. 2007. "Next-generation library catalogs." *Library Technology Reports* (July/August): 15–37. Available: http://web.ebscohost.com (accessed October 9, 2008).

Carlson, Scott. 2005. "Publishers sue Google to prevent scanning of copyrighted works." *Chronicle of Higher Education*, October 28. Available: www.lexisnexis.com/us/lnacademic (accessed October 9, 2008).

Cole, Timothy W., et al. 2002. "Now that we've found the 'hidden Web,' what can we do with it?: The Illinois open archives initiative metadata harvesting experience." Available: www.archimuse.com/mw2002/papers/cole/cole.html (accessed October 9, 2008).

Coyle, Karen. 2006. "Mass digitization of books." *Journal of Academic Librarianship* 32: 641–645. Available: http://vnweb.hwwilson.com (accessed October 9, 2008).

Ding, Li, Tim Finin, Anupam Joshi, Rong Pan, Yun Peng, and Ravan Reddivari. 2005. "Search on the Semantic Web." *Computer* (October): 62–69.

Enth.com. 2008. "About." Available: http://enth.com/About-enth.aspx?Mode=About-enth (accessed October 9, 2008).

Ferguson, Charles. 2005. "What's next for Google?" *Technology Review* 108, no.1: 38–46.

Fisher, Hollice. 2006. "Free books." *Teacher Magazine* 18, no.2: 20. Available: http://web.ebscohost.com (accessed October 9, 2008).

Fyer, Donna. 2004. "Federated search engines." *Online* 28, no.2: 16–19. Available: http://web.ebscohost.com (accessed October 9, 2008).

Gil, Paul. 2008. "What is 'The Invisible Web'?" *Internet for Beginners*. About.com. Available: http://netforbeginners.about.com/cs/secondaryweb1/a/secondaryweb.htm (accessed October 9, 2008).

Google Book Search. 2008. "About Google Book Search: Overview." Available: http://books.google.com/intl/en/googlebooks/about.html (accessed October 9, 2008).

Google Books Library Project. 2008. Homepage. Available: http://books.google.com/googlebooks/library.html (accessed October 9, 2008).

Google Scholar. 2008. "About Google Scholar." http://scholar.google.com/intl/en/scholar/about.html (accessed October 9, 2008).

Guth, Robert A. 2005. "Microsoft to offer digitized books of British Library." *Wall Street Journal*, November 4, Eastern edition.

Hall, Mark. 2007. "Search giants don't wade." *Computerworld* (April 23): 9. Available: http://web.ebscohost.com (accessed October 9, 2008).

Hane, Paula J. 2004. "Project Gutenberg progresses." *Information Today* (May): 28, 52. Available: http://web.ebscohost.com (accessed October 9, 2008).

Illustration of the World Wide Web "content layers": The World Wide Web: Summer 2005. *Internet for Beginners*. About.com. Available: http://netforbeginners.about.com/library/diagrams/n4layers.htm (accessed October 9, 2008).

Internet Archive. 2008. "About IA." Available: www.archive.org/about/about.php (accessed October 9, 2008).

Jacso, Peter. 2007. "North Carolina State and Plymouth State Universities' OPACs and Dialog's PsychINFO." *Online* 131, no.2: 55–57. Available: http://web.ebscohost.com (accessed October 9, 2008).

Kay, Russell. 2006. "Semantic Web." *Computerworld* (February 27): 32. Available: http://web.ebscohost.com (accessed October 9, 2008).

Kirk, Jeremy. 2008. "Without Microsoft, British Library keeps on digitizing." *The New York Times,* May 30. Available: http://www.nytimes.com (accessed October 9, 2008).

Luther, Judy. 2003. "Trumping Google? Metasearching's promise." *Library Journal* (October 1): 36–39. Available: http://web.ebscohost.com (accessed December 8, 2008).

Lyman, Peter, and Hal. R. Varian. 2003. "How much information 2003." School of Information Management and Systems, University of California at Berkeley. Available: http://www2.sims.berkeley.edu/research/projects/how-much-info-2003/internet.htm (accessed October 9, 2008).

O'Leary, Mick. 2005. "Yahoo! goes deep." *Information Today* (November): 39–43. Available: http://web.ebscohost.com (accessed October 9, 2008).

O'Neill, Nancy. 2004. "Open WorldCat pilot: A user's perspective." *Searcher* (November/December): 54–60. Available: http://web.ebscohost.com (accessed October 9, 2008).

Open Archives Initiative: Frequently asked questions (FAQ) 2002. *Open Archives Initiative.* Available: www.openarchives.org/documents/FAQ.html (accessed October 9, 2008).

Orphan, Stephanie. 2004. "ProQuest announces institutional repository service." *College & Research Libraries News* 65: 421.

Price, Gary. 2005. "Yahoo Search Subscriptions brings premium content into Web search." *Search Engine Watch.* Available: http://blog.searchenginewatch.com/blog/050616-000001.

Project Gutenberg. Homepage. Available: http://www.gutenberg.org/wiki/Main_Page?fb_page_id=6428288402& (accessed October 9, 2008).

Ru, Yanbo, and Ellis Horowitz. 2005. "Indexing the Invisible Web: A survey." *Online Information Review* 29: 249–265.

Sherman, Chris. 2005. *Google Power.* New York: McGraw-Hill/Osborne.

Shreeves, Sarah L., Thomas G. Habing, Kat Hagedorn, and Jeffrey A. Young. 2005. "Current developments and future trends for the OAI Protocol for metadata harvesting." *Library Trends* 53: 576–589.

Smith, Peter. 2007. "Life beyond Google: Do alternative search engines measure up?" *Computerworld* (June 21). Available: www.computerworld.com/action/article.do?command=viewArticleBasic&articleId=9025179&pageNumber=4 (accessed October 9, 2008).

Tennant, Roy. 2005. "The Open Content Alliance." *Library Journal* (December 15): 38. Available: http://web.ebscohost.com (accessed October 9, 2008).

University of Rochester's eXtensible catalog project. 2008. Available: www.extensiblecatalog.info/wp-content/uploads/2008/01/XC%20Info%20Sheet.pdf (accessed October 9, 2008).

Yahoo! 2004. For immediate release: Yahoo! Search launches new Content Acquisition Program, providing more relevant, comprehensive online content for users. *Yahoo! Media Relations.* Available: http://docs.yahoo.com/docs/pr/release1144.html (accessed October 9, 2008).

Yahoo! Search Subscriptions. 2008. Homepage. Available: http://search.yahoo.com/subscriptions (accessed October 9, 2008).

Young, Jeffrey R. 2005. "Authors' group sues Google over library-scanning project." *Chronicle of Higher Education,* September 30. Available: http://www.lexisnexis.com/us/lnacademic (accessed October 9, 2008).

►Appendices

►Appendix A
SELECTED ADDITIONAL READINGS

This section does not pretend to be an exhaustive listing of sources on the Invisible Web. It represents additional reading categorized in three sections: Invisible Web/Deep Web, Searching, and User Habits and Culture. These sources are meant to supplement the references listed at the end of each chapter. They are intended to support further reading for those interested in pursuing the Invisible Web in more depth.

INVISIBLE WEB/DEEP WEB

Devine, Jane, and Francine Egger-Sider. 2004. "Beyond Google: The Invisible Web in the academic library." *The Journal of Academic Librarianship* 30: 265–269.

Diaz, Karen. 2000. "The Invisible Web: Navigating the Web outside traditional search engines." *Reference & User Services Quarterly* 40, no.2: 131–134.

Digimind. 2006. "Discover and exploit the Invisible Web for competitive intelligence." White paper. Digimind. Available: www.digimind.com/publications/white-papers/331-discover-and-exploit-the-invisible-web-for-competitive-intelligence.htm (accessed December 16, 2008).

Egger-Sider, Francine, and Jane Devine. 2005. "Google, the Invisible Web, and librarians: Slaying the research Goliath." *Internet Reference Services Quarterly* 10, no.3/4: 89–101. Also co-published in *Libraries and Google*, edited by William Miller and Rita M. Pellen, 89–101. Binghamton, NY: The Haworth Information Press.

Ford, Nigel, and Yazdan Mansourian. 2006. "The invisible Web: An empirical study of 'cognitive invisibility.'" *Journal of Documentation* 62: 584–596.

He, Bin, Mitesh Patel, Zhen Zhang, and Kevin Chen-Chuan Chang. 2007. "Accessing the deep Web: Attempting to locate and quantify material on the Web that is hidden from typical search techniques." *Communications of the ACM* 50, no.5: 95–101.

Henninger, Maureen. 2003. *The Hidden Web: Finding Quality Information on the Net.* Sydney: University of South Wales Press.

Hricko, Mary. 2002. "Using the Invisible Web to teach information literacy." *Journal of Library Administration* 37: 379–386.

Lackie, Robert 2004. "The evolving 'Invisible Web': Tried-and-true methods and new developments for locating the Web's hidden content." *College & Undergraduate Libraries* 10, no.2: 65–71.

Lewandowski, Dirk, and Philipp Mayr. 2006. "Exploring the academic invisible Web." *Library Hi Tech* 24: 529–539.

Ojala, Marydee. 2002. "Mining the deep Web for company information." *Online* 26, no.5: 73–75.

Pedley, Paul. 2001. *The Invisible Web: Searching the Hidden Parts of the Internet.* London: Aslib-IMI.

———. 2002. "Why you can't afford to ignore the Invisible Web." *Business Information Review* 19, no.1: 23–31.

Price, Gary, and Chris Sherman. 2001. "Exploring the Invisible Web." *Online* 25, no.4. Available: http://web.ebscohost.com (accessed December 16, 2008).

Sherman, Chris, and Gary Price. 2001. *The Invisible Web: Uncovering Information Sources Search Engines Can't See.* Medford, NJ: Information Today.

———. 2003. "The Invisible Web: Uncovering sources search engines can't see." *Library Trends* 52: 283–298.

Spencer, Brett. 2007. "Harnessing the deep Web: A practical plan for locating free specialty databases on the Web." *Reference Services Review* 35, no.1: 71–83.

Wouters, Paul, Colin Reddy, and Isidro Arguillo. 2006. "On the visibility of information on the Web: An exploratory experimental approach." *Research Evaluation* 15, no.2: 107–115. Available: http://web.ebscohost.com (accessed December 16, 2008).

Wright, Alex. 2004. "In search of the deep Web." *Salon.com* (March 9). Available: http://dir.salon.com/story/tech/feature/2004/03/09/deep_web (accessed December 16, 2008).

SEARCHING

Arnold, Stephen E. 2003. "In search of . . . The good search: The invisible elephant." *Searcher* 11, no.3. Available: www.infotoday.com/searcher/mar03/arnold.shtml (accessed December 16, 2008).

Beall, Jeffrey. 2007. "Search fatigue: Find a cure for the database blues." *American Libraries* 38, no.3: 46–50.

Bell, Steven J. "The infodiet: How libraries can offer an appetizing alternative to Google." *The Chronicle of Higher Education,* February 20, Supplement.

Bergman, Michael K. 2004. "Why is standard search alone inadequate to meet real business needs?" White Paper. BrightPlanet (December). Available: www.brightplanet.com/resources/details/standard-search-inadequate.htm (accessed December 16, 2008).

Brophy, Jan, and David Bawden. 2005. "Is Google enough? Comparison of an Internet search engine with academic library resources." *Aslib Proceedings* 57: 498–512.

Carlson, Scott. 2003. "New allies in the fight against research by Googling: Faculty members and librarians." *Chronicle of Higher Education,* March 21.

Cohen, Laura B. 2005. "Finding scholarly content on the Web: From Google Scholar to RSS feeds." Special issue. *Choice* 42: 7–17.

Cuil—the world's biggest search engine. 2008. Cuil.com. Available: www.cuil.com/info/.

De Blaaij, Cees de. 2004. "Grey literature from invisibility to visibility." *Publishing Research Quarterly* 20, no.1: 70–76.

Descy, Don E. 2004. "Searching the Web: From the visible to the invisible." *TechTrends* 48, no.1: 5–6. Available: http://web.ebscohost.com (accessed December 15, 2008).

Epstein, Jason. 2006. Books@Google. *The New York Review of Books*, October 19.

Grivell, Les. 2006. "Seek and you shall find?" *EMBO Reports* 7, no.1: 10–13. Available: http://www.nature.com/embor/journal/v7/n1/full/7400605.html (accessed December 15, 2008).

Hagedorn, Kat, and Joshua Santelli. 2008. "Google still not indexing hidden Web URLs." *D-Lib Magazine* 14, no.7/8. Available: http://dlib.org/dlib/july08/hagedorn/07hagedorn.html (accessed December 15, 2008).

Hawkins, Donald T. 2005. "The latest on search engines." *Information Today* 22, no.6: 37–38. Available: http://web.ebscohost.com (accessed December 15, 2008).

Lossau, Norbert. 2004. "Search engine technology and digital libraries: Libraries need to discover the academic Internet." *D-Lib Magazine* 10, no.6. Available: www.dlib.org/dlib/june04/lossau/06lossau.html (accessed December 15, 2008).

Mansourian, Yazdan. 2007. "Methodological approaches in Web search research." *The Electronic Library* 25, no.1: 90–101.

McCown, Frank, Xiaoming Liu, Michael L. Nelson, and Mohammad Zubair. 2006. *Search Engine Coverage of the OAI-PMH Corpus*. Technical report. Los Alamos, NM: Los Alamos National Laboratory. Available: http://library.lanl.gov/cgi-bin/getfile?LA-UR-05-9158.pdf (accessed December 16, 2008).

Mostafa, Javed. 2005. "Seeking better Web searches." *Scientific American* 292, no.2: 67–73. Available: http://web.ebscohost.com (accessed December 15, 2008).

Nielsen, Jakob. 2005. "Mental models for search are getting firmer." *Useit.com* (May). Available: www.useit.com/alertbox/20050509.html (accessed December 15, 2008).

———. 2006. "100 million websites." *Useit.com* (November). Available: www.useit.com/alertbox/web-growth.html (accessed December 15, 2008).

Ortiz Jr., Sixto. 2007. "Searching the visual Web." *Computer* (June): 12–14. Available: http://www.ebscohost.com (accessed December 15, 2008).

Pack, Thomas. 2001. "Getting vertical to cut research time." *Online* 25, no.5: 44–47. Available: http://web.ebscohost.com (accessed December 15, 2008).

Perez, Juan Carlos. 2006. "What is vertical search?" *InfoWorld* (January 18). Available: www.infoworld.com/article/06/01/18/74292_HNverticalsearch_1.html (accessed December 15, 2008).

Price, Gary. 2003. "What Google teaches us that has nothing to do with searching." *Searcher* 11, no.10: 35–37. Available: www.infotoday.com/searcher/nov03/price.shtml (accessed December 15, 2008).

Sherman, Chris. 2005. *Google Power: Unleash the Full Potential of Google*. Emeryville, CA: McGraw-Hill/Osborne.

Smith, Peter. 2007. "Life beyond Google: Do alternative search engines measure up?" *Computerworld* (June 21). Available: www.computerworld.com/action/article.do? command=viewArticleBasic&articleId=9025179&pageNumber=4 (accessed December 15, 2008).

Storey, Tom. 2007. "Search for tomorrow: Preparing for a new age in information gathering." *Nextspace* 6 (April). Available: www.oclc.org/nextspace/006/1.htm (accessed December 15, 2008).

Vine, Rita. 2004. "Going beyond Google for faster and smarter Web searching." *Teacher Librarian* 32, no.1: 19–22. Available: http://web.ebscohost.com (accessed December 16, 2008).

Weetman DaCosta, Jacqui, and Becky Jones. 2007. "Developing students' information and research skills via Blackboard." *Communications in Information Literacy* 1, no.1. Available: www.comminfolit.org/index.php/cil/article/view/Spring2007AR2/33 (accessed December 15, 2008).

USER HABITS AND CULTURE

Ashe, James Casey. 2003. "Information habits of community college students: A literature survey." *Community & Junior College Libraries* 11, no.4: 17–25.

Cothey, Vivian. 2002. "A longitudinal study of World Wide Web users' information-searching behavior." *Journal of the American Society for Information Science and Technology* 53, no.2: 67–78.

Jansen, Bernard J., and Udo Pooch. 2001. "A review of Web searching studies and a framework for future research." *Journal of the American Society for Information Science and Technology* 52, no.3: 235–246.

Murray, Liam, Triona Hourigan, Catherine Jeanneau, and Dominic Chappell. 2005. "Netskills and the current state of beliefs and practices in student learning: An assessment and recommendations." *British Journal of Educational Technology* 36: 425–438.

Spink, Amanda, Dietmar Wolfram, Major B. J. Jansen, and Tefko Saracevic. 2001. "Searching the Web: The public and their queries." *Journal of the American Society for Information Science and Technology* 52, no.3: 226–234.

Strouse, Roger. 2004. "The changing face of content users." *Online* 28, no.5: 27–31. Available: http://web.ebscohost.com (accessed December 16, 2008).

Van Scoyoc, Anna M., and Caroline Cason. 2006. "The electronic academic library: Undergraduate research behavior in a library without books." *portal: Libraries and the Academy* 6, no.1: 47–58. Available: http://muse.jhu.edu/journals/portal_libraries_and_the_academy/v006/6.1van_scoyoc.pdf (accessed December 16, 2008).

Wright, Carol A. 2004. "The academic library as a gateway to the Internet: An analysis of the extent and nature of search engine access from academic library home pages." *College & Research Libraries* 65, no.4: 276–286.

▶Appendix B

TOOLS FOR TEACHING
THE INVISIBLE WEB

Teaching anything, even the Invisible Web, can be enhanced by using graphics, media, and other tools that appeal to students and may make difficult-to-grasp ideas easier to approach. Here are some tools that can add to the classroom teaching experience. They might also be used in conjunction with Web guides and tutorials or Blackboard course sites. This is by no means intended as an exhaustive listing but it may provide a good starting point. (All source information is given to facilitate the permissions process as needed.)

GRAPHICS

A good graphic can go far in helping people understand the place of the Invisible Web in the information world. Probably one of the most important established visual images of the Invisible Web is the one given in Michael K. Bergman's white paper and article "The Deep Web: Surfacing Hidden Value" shown in Chapter 1. His fishing trawler graphic conveys the Web world of information as the ocean and fishing nets as search tools. The ocean clearly holds far more potential than the shallow, surface Web nets can grasp.

Using a similar image of the ocean as the world of information that seems based on Bergman but that furthers the imagery is from the Juanico Environmental Consultants Ltd. Web site (see Figure B-1).

Another effective visual concept for the Invisible Web has always been an iceberg. The "tip of the iceberg" that shows above water and its much greater mass below the water level effectively gives a sense of proportion to the surface and Invisible Webs. It also nicely shows them as parts of the same iceberg or information world. Figure B-2 is an example from the CloserLookSearch.com Web site.

Charts and diagrams have been used to explain the Invisible Web. Charts can be complicated and may require adequate text explanation to help students decipher them. Some examples follow.

▶ **FIGURE B-1: Comparing the Surface Visible Web and the Deep Invisible Web**

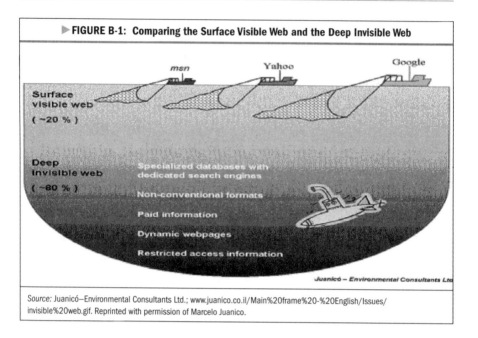

Source: Juanicó–Environmental Consultants Ltd.; www.juanico.co.il/Main%20frame%20-%20English/Issues/invisible%20web.gif. Reprinted with permission of Marcelo Juanico.

▶ **FIGURE B-2: The Tip of the Iceberg**

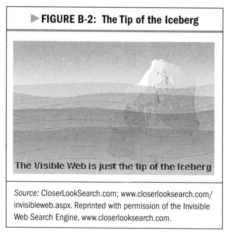

The Visible Web is just the tip of the Iceberg

Source: CloserLookSearch.com; www.closerlooksearch.com/invisibleweb.aspx. Reprinted with permission of the Invisible Web Search Engine, www.closerlooksearch.com.

Figure B-3 is a simple chart that shows surface and Invisible Web attributes.

Another example is Figure B-4, which is based on the description of the Invisible Web as provided by authors Chris Sherman and Gary Price in their book *The Invisible Web: Uncovering Information Sources Search Engines Can't See*, 2001, Cyber Age Books. It was developed by Nigel Ford and Yazdan Mansourian for an article on the Invisible Web.

The U.S. government is a major contributor to the Invisible Web and has been working hard to make its resources more accessible. Two government-generated images are presented in Figure B-5.

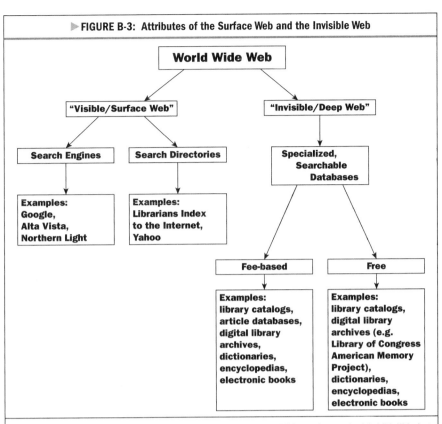

► FIGURE B-3: Attributes of the Surface Web and the Invisible Web

World Wide Web

"Visible/Surface Web"

"Invisible/Deep Web"

Search Engines

Search Directories

Specialized, Searchable Databases

Examples:
Google,
Alta Vista,
Northern Light

Examples:
Librarians Index
to the Internet,
Yahoo

Fee-based

Free

Examples:
library catalogs,
article databases,
digital library
archives,
dictionaries,
encyclopedias,
electronic books

Examples:
library catalogs,
digital library
archives (e.g.
Library of Congress
American Memory
Project),
dictionaries,
encyclopedias,
electronic books

Source: "AT&T Education—21st Century Literacies" http://www.kn.att.com/wired/21stcent/wversus.html. Invisible Web chart created by Stephanie Sterling Brasley. Reprinted with permission.

► FIGURE B-4: The Invisible Web

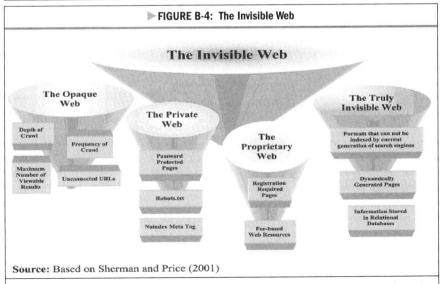

The Invisible Web

The Opaque Web

Depth of Crawl

Frequency of Crawl

Maximum Number of Viewable Results

Unconnected URLs

The Private Web

Password Protected Pages

Robots.txt

Noindex Meta Tag

The Proprietary Web

Registration Required Pages

Fee-based Web Resources

The Truly Invisible Web

Formats that can not be indexed by current generation of search engines

Dynamically Generated Pages

Information Stored in Relational Databases

Source: Based on Sherman and Price (2001)

Source: Ford, Nigel, and Yazdan Mansourian. 2006. "The invisible Web: An empirical study of cognitive invisibility." *Journal of Documentation* 62, no.5: 584–596. Reprinted with permission from Emerald Group Publishing.

> ► **FIGURE B-5: Two Deep Web Images Generated by the U.S. Government**
>
>
>
> *Source:* www.osti.gov/speeches/fy2006/icsti/images/slide6.jpg.
>
>
>
> *Source:* Office of Scientific and Technical Information; www.osti.gov/speeches/fy2005/wlwNSDLNov04_files/images/image5-2.png

> ► **FIGURE B-6: Special Tools Are Needed to Search the Deep Web**
>
>
>
> *Source:* Wright, Alex. 2004 "In Search of the Deep Web"; http://archive.salon.com/tech/feature/2004/03/09/deep_web/print.html. Reprinted with permission. This image first appeared at www.salon.com.

A final category of images conveys the need for special tools to search the Invisible Web, as seen in Figure B-6.

AUDIO AND VIDEO MATERIALS

Take advantage of some of the following streaming media items available on the Web.

Audio

Title: 21st Century Information Fluency Project—MicroModule: Invisible Web
Sponsored by: Illinois Mathematics and Science Academy
Length: Approximately 3 minutes.
Link: http://21cif.imsa.edu/tutorials/micro/mm/invisible/audio/page1.swf

This audio focuses on Invisible Web content and searching tools.

Video

Title: Searching the Deep Web
Sponsored by: Office of Scientific and Technical Information
Length: Approximately 6 minutes
Format: QuickTime or Windows Media Player
Link: www.osti.gov/media/DeepWebVideo

Discusses the need for the Invisible Web in scientific research.

Title: Luminary Lectures @ Your Library: Gary Price and Chris Sherman—Web Research: What's New in 2004
Sponsored by: Library of Congress
Length: 1 hour, 37 minutes
Format: RealPlayer
Link: www.loc.gov/rr/program/lectures/gpcs.html

Although this recorded presentation is about research in general, it does afford the opportunity to hear from the authors regarding the most important book about the Invisible Web.

Title: The Future Just Happened
Sponsored by: BBC News
Length: 1 minute, 43 seconds
Format: RealPlayer
Link: http://news.bbc.co.uk/hi/english/static/in_depth/programmes/2001/future/invisible_web.stm

Paul Pedley, the first author of a book about the Invisible Web, explains its importance.

TUTORIALS/GUIDES

The following guides and tutorials can help serve as class assignments or they can be linked from course Blackboard sites or as library Web site guides. Many good guides available on the Web; these are examples of some of the best.

Title: What Is the Invisible Web?
Sponsored by: 21st Century Information Fluency Project.
Link: http://21cif.imsa.edu/tutorials/micro/mmpdf/invisible.pdf
Title: Invisible or Deep Web: What It Is, Why It Exists, How to Find It, and Its Inherent Ambiguity
Sponsored by: University of California-Berkeley Library
Link: www.lib.berkeley.edu/TeachingLib/Guides/Internet/InvisibleWeb.html

Title: Invisible Web: The Cloaked Internet
Sponsored by: About.com
Link: http://netforbeginners.about.com/od/invisibleweb/Invisible_Web_The_Cloaked_Internet.htm

About.com offers several guides about the Invisible Web. Here is a link that organizes them for easy access.

Title: The Ultimate Guide to the Invisible Web
Sponsored by: Online Education Database
Link: http://oedb.org/library/college-basics/invisible-web

Title: Internet Tutorials: The Deep Web
Sponsored by: Laura Cohen, University of Albany
Link: www.internettutorials.net/deepweb.html

BLOGS

Blogs can have a great appeal for students. Here are two that involve the Invisible Web.

Title: The Invisible Web Weblog: A Weblog About the Invisible Web and Information Available on the Web
Maintained by: Yazdan Mansourian
Link: http://invisibleweblog.blogspot.com

Title: Deep Web Research
Maintained by: Marcus P. Zilman
Link: http://deepwebresearch.blogspot.com

►Appendix C

ACRL INFORMATION LITERACY STANDARDS, PERFORMANCE INDICATORS, AND OUTCOMES

Excerpted from *Information Literacy Competency Standards for Higher Education.* Reprinted with permission of the Association of College and Research Libraries, American Library Association.

STANDARD ONE

The information literate student determines the nature and extent of the information needed.

Performance Indicators:

1. The information literate student defines and articulates the need for information.

   Outcomes Include:

   a. Confers with instructors and participates in class discussions, peer work-groups, and electronic discussions to identify a research topic, or other information need

   b. Develops a thesis statement and formulates questions based on the information need

   c. Explores general information sources to increase familiarity with the topic

   d. Defines or modifies the information need to achieve a manageable focus

   e. Identifies key concepts and terms that describe the information need

   f. Recognizes that existing information can be combined with original thought, experimentation, and/or analysis to produce new information

2. The information literate student identifies a variety of types and formats of potential sources for information.

Outcomes Include:

a. Knows how information is formally and informally produced, organized, and disseminated

b. Recognizes that knowledge can be organized into disciplines that influence the way information is accessed

c. Identifies the value and differences of potential resources in a variety of formats (e.g., multimedia, database, website, data set, audio/visual, book)

d. Identifies the purpose and audience of potential resources (e.g., popular vs. scholarly, current vs. historical)

e. Differentiates between primary and secondary sources, recognizing how their use and importance vary with each discipline

f. Realizes that information may need to be constructed with raw data from primary sources

3. The information literate student considers the costs and benefits of acquiring the needed information.

Outcomes Include:

a. Determines the availability of needed information and makes decisions on broadening the information seeking process beyond local resources (e.g., interlibrary loan; using resources at other locations; obtaining images, videos, text, or sound)

b. Considers the feasibility of acquiring a new language or skill (e.g., foreign or discipline-based) in order to gather needed information and to understand its context

c. Defines a realistic overall plan and timeline to acquire the needed information

4. The information literate student reevaluates the nature and extent of the information need.

Outcomes Include:

a. Reviews the initial information need to clarify, revise, or refine the question

b. Describes criteria used to make information decisions and choices

STANDARD TWO

The information literate student accesses needed information effectively and efficiently.

Performance Indicators:

1. The information literate student selects the most appropriate investigative methods or information retrieval systems for accessing the needed information.

   Outcomes Include:

   a. Identifies appropriate investigative methods (e.g., laboratory experiment, simulation, fieldwork)
   b. Investigates benefits and applicability of various investigative methods
   c. Investigates the scope, content, and organization of information retrieval systems
   d. Selects efficient and effective approaches for accessing the information needed from the investigative method or information retrieval system

2. The information literate student constructs and implements effectively-designed search strategies.

   Outcomes Include:

   a. Develops a research plan appropriate to the investigative method
   b. Identifies keywords, synonyms and related terms for the information needed
   c. Selects controlled vocabulary specific to the discipline or information retrieval source
   d. Constructs a search strategy using appropriate commands for the information retrieval system selected (e.g., Boolean operators, truncation, and proximity for search engines; internal organizers such as indexes for books)
   e. Implements the search strategy in various information retrieval systems using different user interfaces and search engines, with different command languages, protocols, and search parameters
   f. Implements the search using investigative protocols appropriate to the discipline

3. The information literate student retrieves information online or in person using a variety of methods.

   Outcomes Include:

   a. Uses various search systems to retrieve information in a variety of formats
   b. Uses various classification schemes and other systems (e.g., call number systems or indexes) to locate information resources within the library or to identify specific sites for physical exploration
   c. Uses specialized online or in person services available at the institution to retrieve information needed (e.g., interlibrary loan/document delivery,

professional associations, institutional research offices, community resources, experts and practitioners)

   d. Uses surveys, letters, interviews, and other forms of inquiry to retrieve primary information

4. The information literate student refines the search strategy if necessary.

Outcomes Include:

   a. Assesses the quantity, quality, and relevance of the search results to determine whether alternative information retrieval systems or investigative methods should be utilized

   b. Identifies gaps in the information retrieved and determines if the search strategy should be revised

   c. Repeats the search using the revised strategy as necessary

5. The information literate student extracts, records, and manages the information and its sources.

Outcomes Include:

   a. Selects among various technologies the most appropriate one for the task of extracting the needed information (e.g., copy/paste software functions, photocopier, scanner, audio/visual equipment, or exploratory instruments)

   b. Creates a system for organizing the information

   c. Differentiates between the types of sources cited and understands the elements and correct syntax of a citation for a wide range of resources

   d. Records all pertinent citation information for future reference

   e. Uses various technologies to manage the information selected and organized

STANDARD THREE

The information literate student evaluates information and its sources critically and incorporates selected information into his or her knowledge base and value system.

Performance Indicators:

1. The information literate student summarizes the main ideas to be extracted from the information gathered.

Outcomes Include:

   a. Reads the text and selects main ideas

   b. Restates textual concepts in his/her own words and selects data accurately

   c. Identifies verbatim material that can be then appropriately quoted

2. The information literate student articulates and applies initial criteria for evaluating both the information and its sources.

   Outcomes Include:

   a. Examines and compares information from various sources in order to evaluate reliability, validity, accuracy, authority, timeliness, and point of view or bias
   b. Analyzes the structure and logic of supporting arguments or methods
   c. Recognizes prejudice, deception, or manipulation
   d. Recognizes the cultural, physical, or other context within which the information was created and understands the impact of context on interpreting the information

3. The information literate student synthesizes main ideas to construct new concepts.

   Outcomes Include:

   a. Recognizes interrelationships among concepts and combines them into potentially useful primary statements with supporting evidence
   b. Extends initial synthesis, when possible, at a higher level of abstraction to construct new hypotheses that may require additional information
   c. Utilizes computer and other technologies (e.g. spreadsheets, databases, multimedia, and audio or visual equipment) for studying the interaction of ideas and other phenomena

4. The information literate student compares new knowledge with prior knowledge to determine the value added, contradictions, or other unique characteristics of the information.

   Outcomes Include:

   a. Determines whether information satisfies the research or other information need
   b. Uses consciously selected criteria to determine whether the information contradicts or verifies information used from other sources
   c. Draws conclusions based upon information gathered
   d. Tests theories with discipline-appropriate techniques (e.g., simulators, experiments)
   e. Determines probable accuracy by questioning the source of the data, the limitations of the information gathering tools or strategies, and the reasonableness of the conclusions
   f. Integrates new information with previous information or knowledge
   g. Selects information that provides evidence for the topic

5. The information literate student determines whether the new knowledge has an impact on the individual's value system and takes steps to reconcile differences.

Outcomes Include:

a. Investigates differing viewpoints encountered in the literature
b. Determines whether to incorporate or reject viewpoints encountered

6. The information literate student validates understanding and interpretation of the information through discourse with other individuals, subject-area experts, and/or practitioners.

Outcomes Include:

a. Participates in classroom and other discussions
b. Participates in class-sponsored electronic communication forums designed to encourage discourse on the topic (e.g., email, bulletin boards, chat rooms)
c. Seeks expert opinion through a variety of mechanisms (e.g., interviews, email, listservs)

7. The information literate student determines whether the initial query should be revised.

Outcomes Include:

a. Determines if original information need has been satisfied or if additional information is needed
b. Reviews search strategy and incorporates additional concepts as necessary
c. Reviews information retrieval sources used and expands to include others as needed

STANDARD FOUR

The information literate student, individually or as a member of a group, uses information effectively to accomplish a specific purpose.

Performance Indicators:

1. The information literate student applies new and prior information to the planning and creation of a particular product or performance.

Outcomes Include:

a. Organizes the content in a manner that supports the purposes and format of the product or performance (e.g. outlines, drafts, storyboards)
b. Articulates knowledge and skills transferred from prior experiences to planning and creating the product or performance

    c. Integrates the new and prior information, including quotations and paraphrasings, in a manner that supports the purposes of the product or performance

    d. Manipulates digital text, images, and data, as needed, transferring them from their original locations and formats to a new context

2. The information literate student revises the development process for the product or performance.

    Outcomes Include:

    a. Maintains a journal or log of activities related to the information seeking, evaluating, and communicating process

    b. Reflects on past successes, failures, and alternative strategies

3. The information literate student communicates the product or performance effectively to others.

    Outcomes Include:

    a. Chooses a communication medium and format that best supports the purposes of the product or performance and the intended audience

    b. Uses a range of information technology applications in creating the product or performance

    c. Incorporates principles of design and communication

    d. Communicates clearly and with a style that supports the purposes of the intended audience

STANDARD FIVE

The information literate student understands many of the economic, legal, and social issues surrounding the use of information and accesses and uses information ethically and legally.

Performance Indicators:

1. The information literate student understands many of the ethical, legal and socio-economic issues surrounding information and information technology.

    Outcomes Include:

    a. Identifies and discusses issues related to privacy and security in both the print and electronic environments

    b. Identifies and discusses issues related to free vs. fee-based access to information

    c. Identifies and discusses issues related to censorship and freedom of speech

    d. Demonstrates an understanding of intellectual property, copyright, and fair use of copyrighted material

2. The information literate student follows laws, regulations, institutional policies, and etiquette related to the access and use of information resources.

Outcomes Include:

a. Participates in electronic discussions following accepted practices (e.g. "Netiquette")

b. Uses approved passwords and other forms of ID for access to information resources

c. Complies with institutional policies on access to information resources

d. Preserves the integrity of information resources, equipment, systems and facilities

e. Legally obtains, stores, and disseminates text, data, images, or sounds

f. Demonstrates an understanding of what constitutes plagiarism and does not represent work attributable to others as his/her own

g. Demonstrates an understanding of institutional policies related to human subjects research

3. The information literate student acknowledges the use of information sources in communicating the product or performance.

Outcomes Include:

a. Selects an appropriate documentation style and uses it consistently to cite sources

b. Posts permission granted notices, as needed, for copyrighted material

►Index

►About the Authors

Jane Devine has been the Chief Librarian and Department Chair for the LaGuardia Community College Library since 2004. Prior to that appointment she served as LaGuardia's Periodicals/Government Documents/Electronic Resources Librarian for ten years. Before joining the LaGuardia faculty, she worked for the New York Public Library as a Reference Librarian. She received both her MLS degree and her master's in English from St. John's University in New York. As someone very interested in the research process, becoming involved in learning and teaching about the Invisible Web seemed a natural progression. A collaboration with Francine Egger-Sider has resulted in two articles and now a book on the subject.

Francine Egger-Sider has been the Coordinator of Technical Services at LaGuardia Community College, part of City University of New York, since 1989. Previously, she worked at the French Institute/Alliance Française in New York City. She has co-authored two articles on the Invisible Web with Professor Jane Devine: "Beyond Google: The Invisible Web in the Academic Library," published in 2004 in the *Journal of Academic Librarianship*, and "Google, the Invisible Web, and Librarians: Slaying the Research Goliath," in the *Internet Reference Services Quarterly* in 2005. She received her MLS from Columbia University and an MALS in International Studies from the Graduate Center, City University of New York. Francine Egger-Sider is a native of Switzerland and is fluent in English, French, and German.